RESEARCH IN GERMANIC STUDIES

1998-1999

THESES COMPLETED IN 1998 and THESES IN PROGRESS 1998-99

at Universities in Great Britain and Ireland

together with

WORK PUBLISHED IN 1998
by Members of the Conference of University Teachers of German in
Great Britain and Ireland

as known on 1 January 1999

Compiled by

GORDON J. A. BURGESS, STEVEN W. LAWRIE and GUNDULA M. SHARMAN

Published by

THE UNIVERSITY OF ABERDEEN
and the
INSTITUTE OF GERMANIC STUDIES
UNIVERSITY OF LONDON SCHOOL OF ADVANCED STUDY

in association with *GERMAN LIFE AND LETTERS*

on behalf of
THE CONFERENCE OF UNIVERSITY TEACHERS OF GERMAN IN
GREAT BRITAIN AND IRELAND

Institute of Germanic Studies LP 51

UK ISSN 0260-5929

ISBN 0-85457-191-4

CONTENTS

PREFACE

Publication of this, the thirty-second issue of the annual survey of current research in Germanic Studies, provides a welcome opportunity to thank all those who have supplied information for inclusion in it for their continuing support. A special word of thanks is due to those who, as well as furnishing information, have generously presented copies of their theses and published works to the Institute of Germanic Studies, London, for addition to its library. Such gifts form the nucleus of a collection of works by British and Irish Scholars in the field of Germanic Studies, a collection the Institute is hoping to develop systematically as and when circumstances permit.

Thanks to the initiative and financial support of the Editors of *German Life and Letters*, it has again been possible to produce the booklet in a printed version for at least one further year: thus, this booklet has been jointly financed by *German Life and Letters* and the CUTG. In addition, *GLL* have continued to make funds available to create and maintain the version on the World Wide Web, available at <http://www.abdn.ac.uk/~ger042/>. Regrettably, the section on work to be published in the forthcoming year has had to be dropped for this volume: in the current research and publishing climate, this section had grown to occupy almost half the booklet, and concern had been growing about the accuracy of some of the entries as well as about the likelihood of their being published within the given time-scale. Whilst final responsibility for the content (and any remaining errors) rests with the compilers, we should like to thank John Flood for his advice and support throughout the production of this booklet, and the Institute of Germanic Studies for accepting it in their Library Publications series. We should also like to thank Hamish Ritchie, W. A. Kelly and Duncan Large for their perceptive proof-reading of the completed typescript.

This booklet has been compiled from information supplied by Heads of Departments in universities and other institutions in Great Britain and Ireland. Requests for information were sent to some 110 institutions, of which a substantial minority failed to respond, declined to be included this year, or sent in a nil return. The completeness (and therefore usefulness) of the information here must be seen in the light of this response rate. Since *Research in Germanic Studies* is intended primarily to serve as a current-awareness bulletin, it does not give full bibliographical information. It simply aims to tell interested colleagues what is going on in Germanic Studies in Great Britain and in Ireland and where to turn for more information.

Research in Germanic Studies comprises three lists:

THESES COMPLETED IN 1998

This list gives details of theses for which higher degrees have been awarded at British and Irish universities between January and December 1998. Each entry comprises the title of the thesis, degree, university and/or college, and the name of the student.

This list contains details of all theses for higher degrees known to be in progress at British and Irish universities on 1 January 1999. The information given for each entry is as in the first list.

WORK PUBLISHED IN 1998

The information for this list has been supplied by members of the Conference of University Teachers of German in Great Britain and Ireland. Titles of books are followed by the publisher and author. Contributions to collections are indicated by 'In:' followed by the title of the collection, editor(s), publisher, and author (where supplied). Where a work is mentioned more than once, full details are given in the first and/or main entry and a short title is used elsewhere. Titles of articles in periodicals are followed by the name of the periodical, in full or abbreviated form, and the author.

CLASSIFICATION

A LANGUAGE
   1 General linguistics
   2 Germanic languages generally
   3 German language
   4 Dutch language
   5 Scandinavian languages
   6 Yiddish language

B LITERATURE
   1 General and comparative studies
   2 German literature: general studies (incl. specific themes and genres)
   3 German literature:
      3.1 To 1500
      3.2 1500-1700
      3.3 The eighteenth century and the Classical Age
      3.4 The Romantic Age
      3.5 1830-1890
      3.6 1890-1945
      3.7 Post-1945
   4 Dutch literature
   5 Scandinavian literature
   6 Yiddish literature

C HISTORY, SOCIETY, INSTITUTIONS
   1 History, politics, sociology
      1.1 To 1900
      1.2 From 1900
   2 Business and management studies since 1900
   3 The press, the media, the arts

In section B 1 – B 3.7 general works on each period are followed by works by and about individual authors arranged alphabetically. Where the submitting institution has indicated that the subject of a work falls into more than one section, the entry has been duplicated and, similarly, entries for studies of more than one author have been duplicated where the authors fall into different period subdivisions; but for studies of authors within the same period the entry occurs only under the name of the author who comes first in the entry.

ABBREVIATIONS

ABBREVIATIONS OF TITLES OF PERIODICALS, SERIES AND PUBLISHERS

DVjs	*Deutsche Vierteljahrsschrift*
FMLS	*Forum for Modern Language Studies*
GLL	*German Life and Letters*
MLR	*Modern Language Review*
NGS	*New German Studies*
OGS	*Oxford German Studies*
PEGS	*Publications of the English Goethe Society*
ZfdA	*Zeitschrift für deutsches Altertum*
ZfdPh	*Zeitschrift für deutsche Philologie*
YWMLS	*The Year's Work in Modern Language Studies*

ABBREVIATIONS OF UNIVERSITIES AND COLLEGES

Bk	Birkbeck College, London
Glds	Goldsmiths, University of London
IGS	Institute of Germanic Studies, London
KC	King's College London
NUI	National University of Ireland
QMW	Queen Mary and Westfield College, London
RH	Royal Holloway, University of London
TCD	Trinity College, Dublin
UC	University College London
UEA	University of East Anglia
UMIST	University of Manchester Institute of Science and Technology
UWE	University of the West of England, Bristol

THESES COMPLETED IN 1998

A LANGUAGE

A2 Germanic languages generally

Teaching and assessing intercultural competence: a first step towards a syllabus design (MA Anglia) M. McMahon

A 3 German language

The weak verbs of Old High German (PhD Newcastle upon Tyne) C. Bailey

The weak verbs of Old Norse (PhD Newcastle upon Tyne) J. Skinner

Teaching and assessing intercultural competence: a first step towards a syllabus design (MA Anglia) M. McMahon

Landeskunde: its role and functions in the Irish German-language classroom. An empirical study (MA NUI, Maynooth) A. M. Lysaght

The introduction of German to secondary schools in Malaysia and the problems encountered (MA NUI, Maynooth) E. O'Sullivan

A contemporary case of sound change: lenition of German /pf/ and /ts/ from an articulatory phonology perspective (M Phil Cambridge) N. McLelland

A comparison of the teaching of modern languages in primary schools in Scotland and Germany (M Litt Aberdeen) C. McLennan

B LITERATURE

B 2 German literature: general studies (incl. specific themes and genres)

Aspects of comedy in contemporary German drama (PhD Sheffield) G. Pye

B 3 German literature

B 3.1 To 1500

The presentation of authorship in thirteenth-century Middle High German narrative poetry (D Phil Oxford) S. C. Coxon

Rhetorical and musical features in the lyric poems of Hartmann von Aue (PhD Leeds) R. J. Davies

B 3.3 The eighteenth century and the Classical Age

The idea of tolerance and the writings of Goethe (D Phil Oxford) P. E. Kerry

The interdependence of science and literature in Goethe's *Die Wahlverwandt-schaften* (PhD London, KC) O. Taaffe

Humboldt's theory of language (PhD London, KC) E. Stubbs

B 3.4 The Romantic Age

The self and its phantoms: subjectivity and imagination in the writings of E. T. A. Hoffmann (PhD TCD) J. Riou

Designing the female and desiring the feminine: the idea of woman in the works of E. T. A. Hoffmann (PhD Liverpool) E. Bishop

The Romantic magus: initiation and tradition in the new mythology of Novalis, Hoffmann and Fouqué (PhD Manchester) L. Voronov

B 3.5 1830-1890

Men, women and the Melusine: gender and humanity in the novels of Theodor Fontane (M Phil Birmingham) S. Braithwaite

Edith Wharton and German literature (PhD London, UC) M. Mercuri

B 3.6 1890-1945

The literature of political extremism in the Weimar Republic (1918-1933) (PhD Sheffield) M. Fechner

Ambiguity in the narratives of Marieluise Fleisser (M Litt Bristol) C. A. Matthias

Jean sans Terre und Ahasver: zur Geschichte des Ewigen Juden und dessen Bedeutung in Ivan Golls Werk (MA NUI, Galway) M. Carney

Excavating Adolf Loos's cultural criticism (PhD Glasgow) J. Stewart

A comparison of the political essays and fiction of Heinrich and Thomas Mann, with particular reference to *Professor Unrat* and *Der Tod in Venedig* (M Phil Birmingham) H. Richardson

Kurt Tucholsky and France (PhD Nottingham) S. Burrows

Animality, sexuality and madness in the Expressionist novels of Ernst Weiß *Tiere in Ketten* and *Nahar* (M Litt TCD) C. Kehoe

Edith Wharton and German literature (PhD London, UC) M. Mercuri

Freedom, psychology, restoration and morality in the *Novellen* of Stefan Zweig (M Phil Keele) K. Broad

B 3.7 Post-1945

The depiction of the Church in East and West German literature (M Litt Aberdeen) I. Macdonald

Aspects of comedy in contemporary German drama (PhD Sheffield) G. Pye

Sexuality, sorority and subversion: an exploration of the literary depiction of the continuum of German women's relationships (PhD Central Lancashire) A. L. Mitchell

'Was noch nicht sein kann, muß wenigstens immer im Werden bleiben': the prose writing of the 'second generation' of GDR women writers before, during and after the *Wende* (PhD Bath) E. Alldred

Comparative study of Bachmann and Celan in light of the aesthetics of T. W. Adorno (PhD Manchester) C. Gribble

'Hast du ein Gedächtnis?' Memory and the representation of the past in the early narratives of Günter Grass (PhD Southampton) K. Hall

Grass's *Die Blechtrommel* and Rushdie's *Midnight's Children*: an analytical comparison (PhD Birmingham) D. Green

Ethics, politics and community in the work of Heiner Müller (PhD Warwick) A. Griffiths

'Dies Totenhaus Hamburg': dehistorisation and delocalisation in the work of Hans Erich Nossack (PhD Wales, Swansea) R. Jenkins

The exile novels of Erich Maria Remarque (MA NUI, Maynooth) E. Duffy

Storyteller of the night: an introduction to the life and works of Rafik Schami (MA NUI, Galway) S. Nestor

Krankheit und Tod in den Werken Markus Werners (MA NUI, Maynooth) P. Mulkeen

C HISTORY, SOCIETY, INSTITUTIONS

C 1 History, politics, sociology

C 1.1 To 1900

The concept of leadership in the political and cultural discourse of 19th and 20th century Germany (PhD Aston) K. Bradshaw

C 1.2 From 1900

Images of Germany in British public opinion: their relationship to diversities in the development of specific forms of political culture (M Phil Oxford Brookes) M.-L. Luginsland

The status of the book-medium in contemporary Germany. Do the publishing industry and other institutions conceive of a particular image of the book? (M Phil Birmingham) D. Malcolm

The concept of leadership in the political and cultural discourse of 19th and 20th-century Germany (PhD Aston) K. Bradshaw

German business studies (PhD Birmingham) E. Mennerich

1968 and its effects on the development of German political culture in the 1970s and early 1980s (M Phil Birmingham) N. P. Baker

Dissent and compliance in the GDR, 1949-1961 (PhD London, UC) C. Ross

The language of incipient opposition: the discourse of the Party of Democratic Socialism in German politics 1989-1995 (PhD Durham) M. Dennison

Women and the experience of unemployment in East Germany: a case study of Magdeburg (M Phil Keele) V. Beck

The role of the masses in regime transformation: exit, voice and loyalty and the collapse of the GDR (PhD Birmingham) J. Grix

'Queer in Austria': Funktion und Funktionieren sozialer Bewegungen anhand des Beispiels der Lesben- und Schwulenbewegung in Österreich. Eine qualitative Studie (PhD Bath) J. Honauer

Nature and ecology in German social theory (PhD Keele) I. Blühdorn

German-Israeli security co-operation (PhD Birmingham) S. Shpiro

Civil society and 'The East' in contemporary German foreign policy identity (M Phil Birmingham) J. Butcher

German policy formulation with regard to the eastern enlargement of the EU (PhD Birmingham) S. Collins

Germany as a civilian power (PhD Birmingham) H. Tewes

Red Green coalitions in the Federal Republic of Germany (PhD Birmingham) C. Lees

'Ohne Hoffnung können wir nicht leben': atheist modernism and religion in the works of Christoph Hein (PhD Sheffield) H. Wiesemann

Wilhelm Stekel and the early history of psychoanalysis (D Phil Sussex) F. N. Clark-Lowes

C 3   The press, the media, the arts

A Room with a View and *Effi Briest*: a comparative study of their adaptation for film by James Ivory and Rainer Werner Fassbinder (MSc Edinburgh) B. Reed

THESES IN PROGRESS 1998/99

A LANGUAGE

A 1 General linguistics

Language and cultural differences (MA Sussex) C. Graszauer

German *be-* verbs and the Generative Lexicon (PhD UMIST) G. A. Gupta

A study of oppositeness in the lexis of English and German (PhD Manchester) V. Hayes

The lexical field of locomotion in English and German: a comparative synchronic and diachronic study (PhD Manchester) P. Storjohann

An investigation of temporal conceptual relations and their linguistic realization in English and German official aircraft accident reports (PhD Surrey) B. Bajaj

German legal terminology and translation theory (M Phil Sheffield) E. St. John

Linguistic and cultural issues in the integration of 'Rußlandsdeutsch' (M Phil Birmingham) J. Struck-Soboleva

Intercultural communication (M Phil Sheffield) J. Woodin

Conversational analysis and intercultural communication: implications for foreign language teaching (M Phil Sheffield) A. Krengel

Hebrew language contact in Yiddish (D Phil Oxford) C. Zuckermann

German 'Languages for All' provision in higher education: an evaluative case study with particular reference to student drop-out (PhD Newcastle upon Tyne) N. Reimann

Foreign language research and its effect on Irish third-level teaching institutions (PhD NUI, Maynooth) C. Sosa

Identity-generating potential of indigenous bilingualism with special reference to the promotion of Gaelic in Scotland and Sorbian in Germany (PhD Middlesex) K. Gebel

Computer-assisted language learning: its implementation at university level (M Phil Exeter) I. Wonnacott

A 2 Germanic languages generally

Studies in Low German texts 1500-1700 (M Phil London, RH) T. Francis

A study of interlanguage phonology with reference to English speakers learning German (M Phil London, RH) A. Broomfield

Terminology of congenital malformations and its perception by different user groups (PhD Kingston / Imperial College) S. Mühlhaus

Equivalence in scientific and technical translation, with practical reference to German-English (PhD Salford) M. Krein-Kühle

Dialectology – Luxembourg (M Phil Sheffield) J. Edge

A linguistic commentary on Wulfila's Gothic translation of St. Mark's Gospel (M Phil Birmingham) J. Sparling

A 3 German language

Regionalism and the standardisation of the German language: the evidence from 16th-century custumals (PhD Leeds) I. Lamparter

An analysis of female discourse in National Socialism 1924-34 (PhD London, RH) G. Horan

A case study in translation: the Aberdeen doctors (PhD Aberdeen) S. Weyland

The lexical field of locomotion in English and German: a comparative synchronic and diachronic study (PhD Manchester) P. Storjohann

The lexical and syntactic properties of the infinitive in German (PhD Manchester) P. Cook

Models of syntactic description for modern German (M Phil Newcastle upon Tyne) E. Sandaver

Do-support and negation in the history of German (PhD Newcastle upon Tyne) N. Langer

Language attitudes towards Standard German in the Wiesloch area (PhD Manchester) A. Morgan

Language use in Magdeburg (M Phil Newcastle upon Tyne) N. Böheim

Attitudes towards dialect in South Tyrol (PhD Durham) A. Mairhofer

Germanic dialect in the Lorraine area of France (M Phil Greenwich) S. P. Hughes

Analysis of a corpus of contemporary German economics and management discourse (PhD Birmingham) A. Mackison

A comparative study of grammars of German (M Phil Birmingham) A. C. Evans

German *Kabarett* and language learning: creative misbehaviour (PhD London, KC) J. McNally

Britain's policy on business language training within the context of the European Union (MA Anglia) P. Connelly

Discursive constructions of Austrians and 'others' in media texts and images (PhD Bradford) E. El Refaie

Diverging discourses: ideological practices in the German media in East and West after reunification (PhD Strathclyde) S. Schrabback

Analysis of language used in a variety of German music magazines (M Phil Cork)
L. Forde

An analysis of methodological approaches to teaching literature at secondary level in
Ireland (MA NUI, Maynooth) A. Lynch

An analysis of the Leaving Certificate Oral Examination in German (MA NUI,
Maynooth) C. Callaghan

Vokabelarbeit im Kontext der Vermittlung deutscher Grammatik: ein empirischer
Versuch (MA NUI, Maynooth) L. Lohmeier

Some literary translation problems posed by Salman Rushdie's *The Satanic Verses*,
with special reference to a published German translation (PhD St Andrews)
I. Westphal

The vocabulary of Serranus' dictionary (M Litt Newcastle upon Tyne) S. Brett

B LITERATURE

B 1 General and comparative studies

Divine or diabolic causation of disease in medieval German and English literature
(M Litt TCD) J. Byrne

A comparative study of contemporary Swiss and Scottish literature (PhD
Edinburgh) C. Laubscher

Das Irlandbild in der zeitgenössischen schweizerischen Literatur (MA NUI,
Maynooth) H. Hauser

Aspects of French and German women's crime fiction (PhD London, QMW)
N. Barfoot

The throne in the forest: imagery in the *Nibelungenlied* and the *Ramayana*, with
special reference to images of kingship (PhD TCD) P. Dalzell

George Mackay Brown – an Orcadian Thomas Mann? A study of George Mackay
Brown with special consideration of the German influences on his work (PhD
Edinburgh) S. Schmid

The question of madness in E. T. A. Hoffmann's *Der Sandmann* and Mary Shelley's
Frankenstein or the modern Prometheus (PhD Wales, Swansea) K. Preuß

Sophie von La Roche's *Geschichte des Fräuleins von Sternheim* and Richardson's
Clarissa: a case study in eighteenth-century Anglo-German literary relations (D Phil
Oxford) R. Umbach

Virginia Woolf and Christa Wolf: a comparative study on their contributions to the
modern novel (MSc Edinburgh) Y. Nakamuro

B 2 German literature: general studies (incl. specific themes and genres)

The impact of coffee houses on literary style (PhD Edinburgh) M. Keane

Konkrete Poesie (M Phil Cork) B. Griffin

Reworkings in German literature (PhD Aberdeen) G. M. Sharman

Postmodern German writing (M Phil Sheffield) J. Woolley

Women and illness in German women's novels, 1770-1914 (D Phil Oxford) A. C. Richards

Facing AIDS: autobiography, identity, desire, survival in German (language) literature (PhD Cambridge) A.-E. Kurth

Dandyism as a principle of aesthetic composition: a study on Büchner, Kafka and Oswald Wiener (PhD Cambridge) F. M. Knapp

The prose work of Hermann Burger (PhD Warwick) A. Dennis

B 3 German literature

B 3.1 To 1500

The Trinity in selected early Middle High German poems (M Litt Stirling) C. Boultbee

Blood in medieval German literature (PhD Cambridge) B. Bildhauer

The influence of 'caritas' on the chivalric code in medieval French and German literature (M Phil Exeter) L. Chequer

The theme of anger in medieval German literature (PhD London, KC) C. Magner

Love declarations in medieval German narrative literature (M Phil London, KC) H. Odonkor

A study of the figure of Guinevere in medieval German Arthurian literature, with reference to her role in the wider medieval Arthurian tradition (M Phil London, KC) C. Knowles

The presentation of female characters in the narrative works of Hartmann von Aue (M Phil Nottingham) A. Fiddy

The depiction of and attitudes to war in Der Stricker's *Karl der Große* and *Daniel von dem Blühenden Tal* (PhD London, KC) R. E. Kellett

Time in Middle High German narrative literature, with special reference to Wolfram von Eschenbach's *Parzival* (PhD London, KC) J. A. Tiplady

B 3.2 1500-1700

Writing by nuns in German in the early modern period (D Phil Oxford) C. A. Pears

Zeichencarmina and *Epicedia* composed for bereaved parents in the 17th century (D Phil Oxford) A. Linden

The problem of the individual in the seventeenth-century novel (D Phil Oxford) R. Wieder

Self-consciousness in the early novel (M Phil London, UC) J. Bertsch

First-person narration in the early European novel (PhD London, UC) R. Uhrig

Perceptions of the Thirty Years' War in contemporary accounts and in literature (D Phil Oxford) G. Mortimer

The theme of money in German literature (PhD London, UC) R. Wenzel

Dutch cultural influence on Brandenburg-Prussia 1640-1700 (M Phil London, UC) A. Munt

Sebastian Franck's polemic pacifism: analysis of an ethical concept against the background of his contemporaries' resonance (M Phil London, UC) B. Jenkins

Making sense of a changing world: the work of Pamphilus Gengenbach (PhD London, UC) P. Naylor

A critical edition with commentary of Jacob Ruff's *Adam und Heva* (PhD Stirling) J. K. Whitelaw

Glück in the narratives of Georg Wickram (PhD TCD) C. Politis

B 3.3 The eighteenth century and the Classical Age

German Romanticism (D Phil Oxford) M. Garrett

The theme of money in German literature (PhD London, UC) R. Wenzel

The moral tale in France and Germany in the 18th century (PhD Exeter) K. Astbury

The Gothic tale in France and Germany 1770-1820 (PhD Exeter) D. Hall

Presentations of sickness and health in the works of German women writers, 1770-1840 (PhD Exeter) A. I. E. Dworak

The generation of Hellenism: the theoretical framework and the transformation of an aesthetic of the Greek land in the late 18th and 19th centuries (D Phil Oxford) C. M. Guthenkse

The aesthetic and political philosophies of Diderot and Goethe (PhD Aberdeen) A. Neil

The rhetoric of Goethe's *Erlebnislyrik* (PhD London, UC) S. Kelly

The uses and function of myth in Goethe's early works (D Phil Oxford) J. C. Jolle

Goethe's *Wilhelm Meisters Wanderjahre* as a modern novel (PhD London, KC)
A. O'Donnell

Hölderlin's philosophy of the history of religion (PhD London, KC) S. Hölscher

The pursuit of authenticity: contrasting and complementary modes of discourse in the writings of J. M. R. Lenz (D Phil Oxford) J. M. Gibbons

Lessing and the *Sturm und Drang* (PhD Cambridge) K. Ottewell

Pedagogic elements in the fictional and other writings of Johann Carl Wezel (1747-1819) (D Phil Oxford) C. J. Minter

B 3.4 The Romantic Age

The theme of money in German literature (PhD London, UC) R. Wenzel

Individualism as theme in French and German Romanticism (M Phil London, UC)
S. Whittock

Bettina von Arnim as an apostle of Enlightenment: a revised reading of Clemens Brentano's *Frühlingskranz* (PhD Lancaster) T. H. H. Bailey

E. T. A. Hoffmann and the cult of natural magic (PhD Nottingham) R. Elliss

'Das Schöne' und 'das Erhabene' bei E. T. A. Hoffmann (PhD Reading) B. Röder

E. T. A. Hoffmann and nineteenth-century English literature (PhD Keele) P. Bauer

Nationalism, cosmopolitanism and the State of Germany: the politics of Heinrich von Kleist (PhD Birmingham) E. Griffiths

Periphery and perspective in Kleist's work (M Litt TCD) R. Magshamhrain

The female voice in Novalis (PhD TCD) J. Hodkinson

Friedrich Leopold Graf zu Stolberg and his relation to Classicism and Romanticism (PhD Manchester) E. Joshua

Ludwig Tieck and the programmes of Romanticism (PhD Cambridge) R. A. Bown

B 3.5 1830-1890

The theme of money in German literature (PhD London, UC) R. Wenzel

Reflectivity in the nineteenth-century *Bildungsroman* (M Phil London, UC)
M. Potter

Order and anarchy in nineteenth-century Swiss prose writing (PhD London, UC)
M. Bott

The portrayal of family rituals in German literature of the nineteenth and twentieth centuries (M Phil London, UC) B. Lester

Narrative techniques in Austria (D Phil Oxford) A. Hartford

Fiction's cultural shorthand: images of Jews and Judaism in German literature 1848-1914 (D Phil Oxford) H. L. Burdekin

Biedermeier bestiaries and philistine physiognomy: image and word in Biedermeier satire (D Phil Oxford) F. S. Clark

The aesthetics of Georg Büchner (PhD Edinburgh) R. Green

Dandyism as a principle of aesthetic composition: a study on Büchner, Kafka and Oswald Wiener (PhD Cambridge) F. M. Knapp

Dialogism, character and identity in the novels of Theodor Fontane (PhD Cambridge) P. J. Bowman

Gustav von Frank: Drama-Prosa-Lyrik (PhD Cork) C. Rommel

A study of Friedrich Hölderlin's letters (PhD Sheffield) L. Fechner

Philipp Königsmarck (PhD Bristol) J. M. Veale

Nietzsche: language, rhetoric and historical interpretation (PhD Cambridge) C. J. Emden

Evolution and degeneration: Nietzsche and nineteenth-century biologism (PhD Cambridge) G. Moore

Arthur Schopenhauer on tragedy (D Phil Oxford) S. Krüger

'Ein eigenes Unglück': Adalbert Stifter's theory and practice of rewriting (PhD Cambridge) S. A. Strong

Theodor Storm: landscape and topography (PhD Sheffield) H. G. Peters

B 3.6 1890-1945

Neue Sachlichkeit as an art movement (PhD Sunderland) S. Plumb

The discourse of modernity and *Neue Sachlichkeit* (PhD Nottingham) F. Littlejohn

Growing up in the Third Reich: the depiction of youth in National Socialist and exile fiction (D Phil Oxford) A. C. Schmidt-Ott

Sexuality and relationships in utopian and dystopian literature (M Litt TCD) C. Ní Dhubhghaill

The theme of money in German literature (PhD London, UC) R. Wenzel

The portrayal of family rituals in German literature of the nineteenth and twentieth centuries (M Phil London, UC) B. Lester

Aestheticism as cognitive disturbance: a study of English and German prose around 1900 (M Phil London, UC) K. Krosny

The poets of the *Sturmkreis* (PhD London, KC) D. Scheyka

Perceptions of women in the Austrian theatre, 1912-1938 (PhD Exeter) E. E. Smith

German literature of the First World War (PhD Lancaster) G. Klatt

Humanism and German literature of the two World Wars (PhD Keele) J. Daniels

Literature in exile: antifascist writing in Switzerland 1929-39 (D Phil Oxford) L. D. Holmes

Arbeitersprechchöre and National Socialist *Thingspiel* (PhD Sheffield) H.-J. Koch

Benjamin, Bloch and *fin-de-siècle* English aesthetics (PhD Nottingham) B. Mertens

Brecht, Naturalism and Stanislavsky (PhD London, KC) V. Jones

Dandyism as a principle of aesthetic composition: a study on Büchner, Kafka and Oswald Wiener (PhD Cambridge) F. M. Knapp

Carl Einstein and the aesthetics of cubism (M Litt TCD) N. Creighton

Hanns Heinz Ewers and the gothic tradition in German literature (M Litt Oxford) M. A. Müller

Dialogism, character and identity in the novels of Theodor Fontane (PhD Cambridge) P. J. Bowman

The principle of duality in Theodor Fontane's *Effi Briest* (M Phil Cork) Y. Winkler

The reconstruction of identity in exile literature: Anna Gmeyner, Martina Wied and Hermynia Zur Mühlen (D Phil Sussex) A. Hammel

Hofmannsthal and the renewal of Greek myth (PhD Cambridge) P. E. M. Ward

English and Austrian aestheticism: on Oscar Wilde and Hugo von Hofmannsthal (M Phil London, UC) A. Schmäcke

Visionary poets in the German dictatorships: Peter Huchel and Johannes Bobrowski (PhD Manchester) N. Yuille

Aus einem reichen Leben: the memoirs of Dr Alfred Huhnhäuser. A study in autobiography (PhD Stirling) C. Martin

Time, history and modernity in the early work of Ernst Jünger (D Phil Oxford) J. E. J. King

Franz Kafka (PhD Cork) M. Frendo

Kafka's 'amtliche Schriften' (PhD Wales, Swansea) J. Davies

Kafka's metamorphoses: reception and representation (PhD Cambridge) M. G. Guida

A commentary on Kafka's *Der Proceß* (PhD London, KC) K. Wischenkämper

Henry William Katz: the life and work of a German-Jewish writer and journalist in exile (D Phil Oxford) E. R. A. Pedersen

Siegfried Kracauer as cultural critic and Weimar literature (PhD Nottingham) M. Fleischer

The lyric poetry of Karl Kraus (M Litt Edinburgh) L. Brand

Else Lasker-Schüler and Edith Sitwell: a comparative study (M Phil Birmingham) C. Schalle

Gertrud von Le Fort: Christian women writers and the inner emigration (D Phil Oxford) L. H. Saward

The literary relationship between Klaus and Thomas Mann (M Phil Kent) F. Strath

Women figures in Thomas Mann's fiction (M Phil London, UC) G. Valentine

Naturwissenschaft in Thomas Mann's *Der Zauberberg* (M Phil Oxford) M. C. W. Herwig

Buddenbrooks and *The Forsyte Saga* (M Phil London, UC) J. Bolton

'Identification' and 'projection' in selected work of Thomas, Heinrich and Klaus Mann (PhD London, QMW) K. Junker

Theodor Plievier: literature, politics and exile (D Phil Oxford) A. M. Stein

Subjectivity and language in Rilke's work (PhD TCD) D. Downes

Historical revelation in the work of Franz Rosenzweig (D Phil Oxford) D. S. Groiser

'Verkehrte Welt': truth, falsehood and the search for a self in the work of Joseph Roth (PhD Wales, Swansea) J. Hughes

Joseph Roth as mediator between eastern European Jewry and the West (PhD Keele) A. May

Questions of identity in René Schickele's *Hans im Schnakenloch* and *Das Erbe am Rhein* (PhD TCD) A. McGillicuddy

The poetry of Franz Baermann Steiner (PhD London, KC) N. Ziegler

Ernst Toller: from *Einheitsfront* to *Volksfront* (PhD Stirling) J. Fotheringham

Friedrich Torberg and the Jewish *Kaffeehauskultur* of twentieth-century Vienna (PhD London, KC) S. Hart

B 3.7 Post-1945

The portrayal of family rituals in German literature of the nineteenth and twentieth centuries (M Phil London, UC) B. Lester

Humanism and German literature of the two World Wars (PhD Keele) J. Daniels

The presentation of a lost war: 1939-1945 in post-war West German popular prose (PhD Stirling) M. Sargeant

Post-1945 Swiss drama (M Litt Bristol) M. D. Ford

Forms of literary assent and dissent in the 20th-century German dictatorships (PhD Manchester) M. Philpotts

Humour in Jewish writing on the Holocaust (MA NUI, Galway) M. Christie

Romanfiguren als Mütter von heranwachsenden Kindern in deutschsprachigen Romanen von Schriftstellerinnen zwischen 1970 und 1985 (M Litt Strathclyde) S. Purshouse

Motherhood in German women's writing of the 1970s and 1980s (PhD Wales, Swansea) E. Jeremiah

Courting Bluebeard: *Märchen* in recent literature in German by women (D Phil Oxford) M. P. Davies

'In diesem besseren Land': developments and debates in GDR poetry 1961-1969 (PhD Leeds) M. Pearce

The lyrics of German-language singer-songwriters and rock musicians since the 1970s (PhD Wales, Swansea) A. Blühdorn

'Scherz, Satire, Ironie und tiefere Bedeutung': the '68 generation is coming home (PhD Wales, Swansea) B. Blüm

The lost eastern territories in post-war German literature and *Vergangenheitsbewältigung* (PhD Wales, Swansea) C. George

Neue Subjektivität in the West German fiction of the 1970s and 1980s (PhD London, KC) J. Leal

GDR cultural policies of the 60s and 70s and children's literature (PhD Manchester) S. Warnecke

Wendesprache (PhD St Andrews) N. Barber

Representations of history in GDR women's writing (D Phil Oxford) H. R. Bridge

The crisis of the subject in recent GDR women's writing (PhD London, UC) J. Barrett

Development in narrative form in recent GDR women's writing (D Phil Oxford) L. Marven

The *Ankunft*-motif in East German prose since unification (PhD Aberdeen) K. Langer

Naive Unschuld und gewitztes Spiel: vom autobiographischen Schreibanlaß zu 'naiven' und 'pikaresken' Erzählstrategien in Texten der Nachwendeliteratur (PhD Bradford) T. Nause

The role of the poet after the *Wende* as represented in poetry by ex-GDR poets 1989-1995 (D Phil Oxford) R. J. Owen

The impact of the *Wende* on contemporary German literature (PhD Edinburgh) K. Stein

Post-*Wende* retrospection: intellectuals reassess the GDR (PhD Nottingham) S. Pearce

Problems of identity in the work of Jewish writers of the former GDR (PhD London, KC) J. Ross

Ethnic Germans in Eastern Europe: a literary study (M Phil London, UC) H. Morrison

Intertextuality in contemporary fiction (M Phil London, UC) M. Symons

Postmodern German writing (M Phil Sheffield) J. Woolley

The political literature of German unification (PhD Reading) C. Bishop

National identity in contemporary Austrian drama (PhD Nottingham) M. Saville

Effects of anti-communism on Austrian cold-war literature (D Phil Oxford) E. L. Pennebaker

A comparative study of contemporary Swiss and Scottish literature (PhD Edinburgh) C. Laubscher

Cabaret and alternative theatre in contemporary Berlin (M Phil Sheffield) R. Bland

Theatre and reunification: adaptations and productions of the classical repertoire on the recent German stage (PhD Sheffield) H. Harnisch

Developments in working-class drama and the *Volksstück* (PhD Sheffield) M. Karpinski

Performance and protection: profiles of *Kind(heit)* and *Kindlichkeit* in Ingeborg Bachmann's prose (PhD Cambridge) K. E. McAuley

Feminine conflicts in the works of Ingeborg Bachmann and Annette von Droste-Hülshoff (PhD Cork) B. Cronin

Ernst Barlach reception (PhD Wales, Swansea) C. Handford

The dramatic texts of Konrad Bayer (PhD Cork) T. Scott

Communication and hope in Bernhard's later prose writings (D Phil Oxford) P. S. Darukhanawala

T. Bernhard's lyrical poetry (PhD Sunderland) D. Kelly

A study of Thomas Bernhard's dramas (M Phil London, UC) I. Maliye

The aesthetics of Thomas Bernhard's prose (M Phil London, UC) L. Pugh

Peter Bichsel and Gerhard Richter: a comparative analysis (M Phil Birmingham) B. Chasemore

Wolf Biermann: themes, motifs and forms (PhD Lancaster) M. Bilkau

Heinrich Böll (PhD Sunderland) G. Breitenbach

Volker Braun: private relationships in a public world (PhD Lancaster) M. Delaney

Brecht, Naturalism and Stanislavsky (PhD London, KC) V. Jones

George Mackay Brown – an Orcadian Thomas Mann? A study of George Mackay Brown with special consideration of the German influences on his work (PhD Edinburgh) S. Schmid

Dissidence and social criticism in the work of Günter de Bruyn (PhD London, KC) C. Lewis

Frank Castorf's political theatre (PhD Sheffield) K. Bargna

'My hope is in the East': Paul Celan's translations from Russian and their relevance in his search for a new poetic language (PhD Cambridge) A. Reali

Reading the post-Holocaust lyric: a study of the lyric poetry of Celan, Ausländer and Sachs (PhD Cambridge) B. J. Thomson

Body and language: texts by Anne Duden and Elfriede Jelinek (PhD Warwick) T. Ludden

'Mit einem Ende beginnt es und endet mit einem Anfang': history, mysticism and nature in the works of Gerd Gaiser (PhD Wales, Swansea) S. Smith

Günter Grass and Germany (M Litt Bristol) R. G. Pike

The motif of food in the works of Günter Grass (PhD Cork) G. Schneider

Representations of cultural encounters in the works of Günter Grass (M Phil Cork) E. Connolly

Political 'engagement' in literary works by Günter Grass and Uwe Johnson (M Phil Cork) U. Duggan

Patterns of conformity in the prose fiction of Christoph Hein (PhD Wales, Swansea) D. Clarke

Modernist awareness and responses to socio-political change in the work of Christoph Hein (PhD Bath) S. Bevan

Taking sides: Stefan Heym's historical fiction (PhD Cambridge) M. E. B. Tait

The theme of taboo in the works of Wolfgang Hilbig (PhD Birmingham) P. Cooke

A study of Ulrich Holbein (PhD Wales, Swansea) P. Derrington

Narrative strategies in Marxist-feminist novels: Elfriede Jelinek and Irmtraud Morgner (D Phil Oxford) E. A. Clements

Double bind: the construction of female subjectivities in the works of Elfriede Jelinek, Christa Reinig and Anne Duden (PhD Oxford Brookes) J. Lanyon

Ernst Jünger and right-wing aesthetics in contemporary Germany (M Phil Sheffield) P. Stear

German nationality and identity before and after the *Wende*: a study of the work of Helga Königsdorf (M Phil / PhD Bath) D. Alberghini

The poetry of Dieter Leisegang (PhD London, KC) C. Oppler

The works of Erich Loest (PhD Wales, Swansea) S. Evans

Music, history, ontology: on Thomas Mann's *Doktor Faustus* (PhD London, UC) R. Pratt

Monika Maron (M Phil Cork) K. Power

The novels of Anna Mitgutsch (PhD Bangor) K. Evans

Narration in the fictional works of Irmtraut Morgner (PhD Nottingham) R. H. Terry

Inheritance, influence, intelligence: Irmtraud Morgner and the politics of culture (D Phil Oxford) G. E. Westgate

Narratives of knowledge in the work of Irmtraud Morgner (PhD Lancaster) G. Plow

Personal and social identity in recent women's writing (Müller, Moníková) (PhD London, UC) S. Goodchild

The poetics of Elisabeth Reichart (PhD Nottingham) L. Ovenden

Uwe Saeger's prose writing of the 1970s and 1980s (PhD Nottingham) J. Seifert

A critical study of Anna Seghers' life and career in the GDR (M Phil / PhD Bath) B. Morgan

The dramas of Kerstin Specht (PhD Edinburgh) C. Reissenberger

The poetry of Franz Baermann Steiner (PhD London, KC) N. Ziegler

The work of Yoko Tawada (PhD Sheffield) S. Fischer

The development of Christa Wolf's political thought as reflected in selected writings (MSc Edinburgh) F. Lunny

Images of utopia in Christa Wolf's *Sommerstück* (PhD Salford) C. Colton

Virginia Woolf and Christa Wolf: a comparative study on their contributions to the modern novel (MSc Edinburgh) Y. Nakamuro

Characterisation of the woman in the works of Christine Wolter, Monika Maron and Helga Königsdorf (PhD Limerick) D. Gaffney

B 4 Dutch literature

The geographical world-view of Jacob van Maerlant (M Litt TCD) L. Schreel

B 6 Yiddish literature

Yiddish women poets between the wars (D Phil Oxford) L. A. Jenschke

Studies in the history of the Hebrew book (D Phil Oxford) B. S. Hill

Tradition and innovation in the ballads of Itsik Manger (D Phil Oxford) H. F. Beer

C HISTORY, SOCIETY, INSTITUTIONS

C 1 History, politics, sociology

C 1.1 To 1900

German national identity (PhD Sheffield) K. Wilds

C 1.2 From 1900

Cosmopolitanism, nationhood and regional identity in Germany, 1800 to the present day (PhD Aston) E. Szantho

Concepts of citizenship in nineteenth-century Germany (PhD London, UC) B. de la Serna-Lopez

Aspects of German gender studies (M Phil Sheffield) S. Thompson

Identity-generating potential of indigenous bilingualism with special reference to the promotion of Gaelic in Scotland and Sorbian in Germany (PhD Middlesex) K. Gebel

Das England-Bild im Wiener *Fin de Siècle* (PhD Aston) E. Ertl

Youth, 'nature' and 'community' in Britain and Germany 1916-1936 (PhD Birmingham) M. Mertens

French-German relations during the collaboration period (PhD Sunderland) J. Streeter

The *Ordnungspolizei* and the Holocaust (M Phil London, RH) F. Dierl

The barbarisation of front-line German infantry divisions in Russia, 1941-43 (PhD Birmingham) B. Shepherd

Comparative study of the manpower management in the aeronautical industry in Britain and Germany during the Second World War (M Phil London, RH) F. Hintzke

Austrian identity and the effects of National Socialism on political discourse (PhD Cambridge) M. Y. Kuypers

Social authoritiarianism and the Left (PhD Sheffield) P. Thompson

Intellectual origins and legacy of the Free German Youth (PhD Sheffield) J. Rhys

Trade union and labour relations in Germany and Poland (PhD Sheffield) C. Annesley

Church and State in the GDR in the 1960s (M Phil London, UC) M. Thomas

Youth, the Church, writers, women and the State in the GDR 1971-1989 (M Phil London, UC) J. Madarász

Contemporary visual arts in Germany, East and West, and the problem of cultural unification (PhD Birmingham) J. Hawksley

The conciliar process and the *Wende* in the GDR (PhD Reading) S. Brown

Unifying women? Experiences and meanings of German unification (PhD Nottingham Trent) C. A. Basten

German unification: an examination of the English and German press coverage from November 1989 to October 1990 (M Litt TCD) C. Doris

An examination of the impact of Victor Gollancz' *Save the Children Project* in post-war Germany (M Litt TCD) L. Kavanagh

Bündnis 90 / Die Grünen: A case study of political alliances in Brandenburg 1990/1994 (PhD UWE) B. Harper

German construction industry (PhD Birmingham) M. Clayson

The relationship between governments and multilateral corporations with reference to Japanese and German industry in the UK (PhD Birmingham) H. Loewendahl

The structural impact of multinational investment (PhD Birmingham) A. McLintock

Germany in the age of crisis management (PhD Birmingham) A. Hoffmann

Comparing German and British political culture through values: an analysis of the values of health care reform (PhD Aston) D. Pritchard

The development of conservative and extreme right-wing thought in Germany from the inception of the unified state to the present (PhD Birmingham) A. Statham

The nature and origin of democratic liberalism in the Federal Republic of Germany since 1945 (PhD Aston) M. Cupples

Pollution and socialism: the environment as a political issue in eastern Germany 1980-1997 (M Litt Bristol) L. R. Quinn

Non-conformity amongst East German youth (PhD London, UC) M. Fenemore

The transformation of the PDS (PhD Birmingham) T. Oppenkowski

PDS women: memories of life in the GDR (PhD Bradford) P. L. Beimborn-Taylor

Comparison of political culture in East and West German women (M Phil Birmingham) D. Wagener

Political culture and societal transformation: the case of Erfurt (PhD Birmingham) N. Hubble

Foreign direct investment: a comparison of Germany and the UK (PhD Birmingham) B. Hamburg

Comparative study of policies for local economic development in the UK and Germany (PhD Birmingham) H. Tooze

Economic transformation and British investment in East Germany (PhD Keele) K. Sucher

Germany's foreign cultural policy post-reunification (PhD Birmingham) M. Fleming-Froy

The constitutional embeddedness of German European policy (M Phil Birmingham) B. Ruppert

Eastern enlargement of the EU: British, German, Czech and Polish perspectives (PhD Birmingham) M. Zaborowski

Germany, the UK and the next EU enlargement (PhD Birmingham) S. Philip

Germany and the eastern enlargement of NATO (PhD Birmingham) N. Thomas

German and Russian views on European security (PhD Birmingham) O. Schütt

European police co-operation: a case study (PhD Aberdeen) A. Naughton

The role of subnational government in the EU policy process: the case of the structural funds in Germany, Spain and the UK (PhD Birmingham) A. Reilly

Lobbying, forms of representation of interests (PhD Birmingham) O. Deiters

The construction of identity in the *Land Hessen* (PhD London, UC) S. Parr

German Liberal Parties in transition (PhD Aberdeen) D. Langston

A critical review of Konrad Adenauer's final years in office (MA Kent) D. Senior

C 2 Business and management studies since 1900

German business and the New Right (PhD Sheffield) D. Phillips

Ethics in purchasing (PhD London, KC) L. Preuss

Britain's policy on business language training within the context of the European Union (MA Anglia) P. Connelly

German corporate culture across linguistic and national borders (PhD Aston) N. O'Mahony

Analysis of a corpus of contemporary German economics and management discourse (PhD Birmingham) A. Mackison

C 3 The press, the media, the arts

The *Lied* Theory of the First Berlin School (1753-68) (PhD Bristol) L. James

Diverging discourses: ideological practices in the German media in East and West after reunification (PhD Strathclyde) S. Schrabback

German unification: an examination of the English and German press coverage from November 1989 to October 1990 (M Litt TCD) C. Doris

Left critique of *Bildzeitung* in the 1970s (PhD Limerick) O. Prendergast

The internet and European culture (PhD Sunderland) C. Mansfield

Der britische Löwe: ein Vorbild für den deutschen Michel? Das stereotype Englandbild in deutschen Zeitschriften zwischen den beiden Weltkriegen (PhD Nottingham Trent) B. S. Jung

Sight, sense and screen: the phenomenology of vision in European avant-garde film (PhD Edinburgh) D. Macrae

Doppelgänger in early cinema (MSc Edinburgh) B. Rashidi

The Double in Wilhelmine cinema, 1895-1914 (PhD Warwick) R. Kiss

Dracula's descendants: on the genealogy of an archetype of West-European and American cinema (PhD Edinburgh) R. Man

Gendered and national identity in DEFA films (PhD Nottingham) J. Gregson

The standing in Great Britain of the German cinema after 1945 (PhD Reading) J. Lembach

The reception of American and West German films in the GDR 1970-1989 (PhD Reading) R. Stott

Female images and gender relations in DEFA films (PhD Reading) A. Rinke

Representation of young people in the films of Helmut Dziuba (M Phil / PhD UWE)
G. Müller

The interplay of media: Rainer Werner Fassbinder's films (PhD Edinburgh)
U. Militz

Caspar David Friedrich: art, philosophy, nature and the inner self (MA NUI,
Galway) S. Egan

Nosferatu: a comparative study of Murnau's and Werner Herzog's films (PhD
Edinburgh) E. V. Ballin

'Utopie Kino': on Edgar Reitz' contributions to the aesthetics of film (PhD
Edinburgh) M. Sobhani

The films of Jean-Marie Straub and Danièle Huillet (PhD Edinburgh) U. Böser

Sound and image in Wim Wenders' films (PhD Edinburgh) A. Graf

Photography and film: their interrelation in the work of Wim Wenders (PhD
Edinburgh) E. Donoghue

WORK PUBLISHED IN 1998

A LANGUAGE

A 1 General linguistics

Luxembourg and the European schools. In: *Beyond bilingualism: multilingualism and multilingual education*, ed. J. Cenoz & F. Genesee (Multilingual Matters) C. Hoffmann

Das Gerüst des Lexikons. Überlegungen zu den organisierenden Prinzipien im Lexikon. In: *Akten des 32. Linguistischen Kolloquiums, Kassel 1997*, ed. H. O. Spillmann & I. Warnke (Lang) P. R. Lutzeier

Agreement and pro-drop in some dialects of English (*Linguistics*) K. Borjars & C. Chapman

A subject-verb agreement hierarchy: evidence from analogical change in modern English dialects. In: *Current issues in linguistic theory: historical linguistics 1995*, ed. R. M. Hogg & L. van Bergen (Benjamins) C. Chapman

Multimedia für kommunikative und interkulturelle Kompetenz (*Info-DaF*) G. Rings

Skopos theory. In: *Encyclopedia of translation studies*, ed. M. Baker (Routledge) C. Schäffner

Translation and quality (Multilingual Matters) ed. C. Schäffner

Translation and norms (Multilingual Matters) ed. C. Schäffner

Qualification for professional translators: translation in language teaching versus teaching translation. In: *Translation and language teaching: language teaching and translation*, ed. K. Malmkjaer (St Jerome) C. Schäffner

Machine translation – ten years on: an overview of the conference. In: *Machine translation – ten years on: proceedings of an international conference held at the University of Cranfield 12-14 November 1994*, ed. A. Vella & D. Clarke (Cranfield University Press) D. R. Lewis

Machine translation today: a critical look at current desktop systems (*The Linguist*) D. R. Lewis

Gesprochene Sprache als Gegenstand des Grammatikunterrichts (*Info-DaF*) G. Reershemius

Echte, falsche oder gar *heimtückische* Freunde? Ein Kommentar zur Metaphorik der Beschreibung von Entlehnungen (*Sprachreport*) A. Musolff

'Data modelling' for contrastive valency lexicography. In: *Mutual exchanges: Sheffield-Münster Colloquium I*, ed. R. J. Kavanagh (Lang) G. A. Gupta

Variation im Deutschen: soziolinguistische Perspektiven (de Gruyter) S. Barbour & P. Stevenson

Einführung in die germanistische Linguistik, H. Gross, 3rd rev. edn. (Iudicium)
K. Fischer

Traducció i context. In: *De l'activitat traductora i literària*, ed. J. Verdegal (Anuari de l'Agrupació Borriarenca de Cultura) J. Boase-Beier

Leerstellen und Störstellen: der postkommunistische Diskurs in Mitteleuropa. In: *Fahnenwörter der Politik – Kontinuität und Brüche*, ed. O. Panagl (Böhlau)
S. Marten-Finnis

Language teaching and learning: current trends in Higher Education (FMLS / OUP)
ed. S. Hotho

Language teaching and learning: a modern relationship. In: *Language teaching and learning...* S. Hotho

Learner motivation – from dilemma to dialogue. In: *Language teaching and learning...* S. Hotho & N. Reimann

Spontaneous spoken language: syntax and discourse (OUP) J. Miller & R. Weinert

'You can say "you" to me': Kohl, Mole and related problems of cultural transfer. In: *Cultural negotiations: Sichtweisen des Anderen*, ed. T. Seidel & C. Brown (Francke) I. F. Roe

How universal is metaphor? The case of drugs in European languages (*Lexicology*)
R. Trim

The translator and the dictionary: beyond words? In: *Using dictionaries: studies of dictionary use by language learners and translators*, ed. B. T. S. Atkins (Niemeyer)
M. A. Rogers & K. Ahmad

Grundlagenprobleme der Sprachwissenschaft: kritische Analyse und Abwägung der allgemeinen Ansichten über Sprache von Saussure, Chomsky und Piaget (Hartung-Gorre) R. A. Hartmann

The bi-cultural classroom: more German-Irish experiences. In: *Intercultural communication and language learning*, ed. D. Ó'Baoill & A. Chambers (IRAAL)
J. Fischer

More than mere words: aims in modern language teaching (*Steiner Education*)
G. M. Sharman

A 2 Germanic languages generally

Lëtzebuergesch. In: *Encyclopedia of the languages of Europe*, ed. G. Price (Blackwell) G. Newton

Gothic; Crimean Gothic; German; Germanic. In: *Encyclopedia of the languages of Europe...* J. West

A Germanic virginity or Teutonic virility? Attitudes to language among earlier German purists. In: *London German Studies VI*, ed. E. M. Batley (IGS)
W. J. Jones

The German language in Switzerland: multilingualism, diglossia, and variation (Lang) F. J. Rash

Parallel texts in translation. In: *Unity in diversity? Current trends in translation studies*, ed. L. Bowker, M. Cronin, D. Kenny & J. Pearson (St Jerome) C. Schäffner

Metaphern. In: *Handbuch Translation*, ed. M. Snell-Hornby, H. G. Hönig, P. Kussmaul & P. A. Schmitt (Stauffenburg) C. Schäffner

Thematisation in English LSP texts in the context of LSP translation. In: *LSP identity and interface: research, knowledge and society*, ed. L. Lindquist, H. Picht & J. Qvistgaard (LSP Centre, Copenhagen Business School) M. A. Rogers

A 3 German language

The case for language / linguistic studies. In: *German studies: old and new challenges. Undergraduate programmes in the United Kingdom and the Republic of Ireland*, ed. P. R. Lutzeier (Lang) P. R. Lutzeier

German *ab initio*: the German Department as a mere language school? In: *German studies: old and new challenges...* P. Wend

Dramapädagogisch lehren und lernen. In: *Praktische Handreichung für Fremdsprachenlehrer*, ed. U. O. H. Jung (Lang) M. L. Schewe

Dramapädagogischer lehren und lernen: eine kurze Einführung in ein neueres didaktisch-methodisches Konzept für den fremdsprachlichen Deutschunterricht (*PerVoi*) M. L. Schewe

Emotion und Kognition im Fremdsprachenunterricht: eine dramapädagogisch-ästhetische Perspektive (*Materialien Deutsch als Fremdsprache*) M. L. Schewe

Emotionen, Fremdwahrnehmung und Fremdspracherwerb. In: *Lern- und Studienstandort Deutschland. Emotion und Kognition. Lernen mit neuen Medien. Materialien Deutsch als Fremdsprache*, ed. A. Wolf & D. Eggers (Fachverband Deutsch als Fremdsprache) U. Aifan

Interkulturelle Begegnung verstehen: ein dramapädagogischer Unterrichtseinstieg anhand eines literarischen Textes. In: *SchauForum oder spielerisches Deutschlernen* (Goethe-Institut Montreal) M. L. Schewe

Fremdsprache inszenieren (*Fremdsprachenunterricht*) M. L. Schewe

Orientation in spoken language: deixis, discourse and modality. In: *Mutual exchanges...* R. Weinert

Hugo's advanced German course (Hugo) S. B. Martin & J. Martin

Willkommen! The new course in German for adult beginners (Hodder & Stoughton) P. Coggle & H. Schenke

Teach yourself German (Hodder & Stoughton) P. Coggle & H. Schenke

Stereotype im Fremdsprachenunterricht (Lang) ed. M. Löschmann & M. Stroinska

Stereotype, Stereotype und kein Ende. In: *Stereotype im Fremdsprachen-unterricht*... M. Löschmann

Them and us: on cognitive and pedagogical aspects of the language-based stereotyping. In: *Stereotype im Fremdsprachenunterricht*... M. Stroinska

Zu Stereotypen in der Fachsprache der Medizin: Problematik und Polaritäten. In: *Stereotype im Fremdsprachenunterricht*... S. Mühlhaus

Zum Problem des sprachlichen Kontinuums im Deutschen (*Zeitschrift für germanistische Linguistik*) M. Durrell

Variation im Deutschen: soziolinguistische Perspektiven (de Gruyter) S. Barbour & P. Stevenson

Sprache und Nation im deutschsprachigen Raum aus der Sicht der englisch-sprachigen Wissenschaft. In: *Sprache und bürgerliche Nation*, ed. D. Cherubim, S. Grosse & K. J. Mattheier (de Gruyter) S. Barbour

Medical terminology and its perception by different user groups. In: *LSP identity and interface*... S. Mühlhaus

Gramática funcional y sus aplicaciones (Estudios de Liguística Aplicada) ed. C. Fandrych & U. Tallowitz

Presentación. In: *Gramática funcional y sus aplicaciones*... C. Fandrych & U. Tallowitz

Fraseología: una propuesta para su tratamiento en el salón de clase. In: *Actas del 9° Encuentro Nacional de Profesores de Lenguas*, ed. A. Ortiz   C. Fandrych & E. Elorduy

Fünf Thesen zur Behandlung von Werbesprache im DaF-Unterricht (*Lebende Sprachen*) G. Rings

Donatella di Cesare: die Sprache in der Philosophie von Karl Jaspers (*MLR*) S. Kirkbright

Continuity and change: German discourse after unification. In: *Political discourse in transition in Europe 1989-1991*, ed. P. Chilton, M. Ilyin & J. Mey (Benjamins) C. Schäffner & O. Porsch

Wirtschaftsdeutsch: neue Herausforderungen – neue Strategien (Sheffield Hallam University Press) ed. S. C. Tebbutt, S. Tietze & J. Bowden

Multimedia Projekte: Studienmodule für Wirtschaftsdeutsch. In: *Wirtschafts-deutsch*... G. Hogan-Brun & R. Whittle

Standortproblematik und die deutsche Wirtschaftswelt: ein integrierter Seminar-ansatz. In: *Wirtschaftsdeutsch*... S. C. Tebbutt

The potential of multi-media for foreign language learning: a critical evaluation (*Computers and the Humanities*) G. Hogan-Brun & R. Whittle

Für Sie gelesen: Alois Wierlacher *Kulturthema Toleranz (Info-DaF)* U. Aifan

DaF in Nigeria. Kulturgeprägte Unterrichtsbedingungen, kulturangemessene Unterrichtsmethoden und subjektive Lehrtheorien von DaF-Lehrkräften in Nigeria *(Jahrbuch für internationale Germanistik)* A. Witte

B LITERATURE

B 1 General and comparative studies

London German Studies VI... ed. E. M. Batley

Cousins at one remove: Anglo-German studies 2 (Northern Universities Press) ed. R. F. M. Byrn

The case for specialist studies: Swiss studies. In: *German studies: old and new challenges...* M. J. Pender

Spectaculum europaeum: theatre and spectacle in Europe 1580-1750. A handbook (Harrassowitz) ed. P. Béhar & H. Watanabe-O'Kelly

Opera in the Iberian Peninsula. In: *Spectaculum europaeum...* H. Watanabe-O'Kelly

From Gaelic to Romantic: Ossianic translations (Rodopi) ed. F. Stafford & H. Gaskill

National myth in 19th-century England and Germany *(The Ethical Record)* M. Oergel

Der neuzeitliche Teufel als entfernter Verwandter des Hephaistos? In: *Festschrift für Renate Boeschenstein,* ed. M. Stern *et al.* (Athenäum) E. Sagarra

The return of King Arthur and the Nibelungen: national myth in nineteenth-century English and German literature (de Gruyter) M. Oergel

Deutsch-irische Verbindungen: Geschichte – Literatur – Übersetzung. Irish-German connections: history – literature – translation (Wissenschaftlicher Verlag Trier) ed. J. Fischer, G. Holfter & T. E. Bourke

Reception theory or preception theory? In: *The systemic and empirical approach to literature and culture as theory and application,* ed. S. T. de Zepetnek & I. Sywenky (LUMIS) H. de Berg

Sinn und Unsinn einer systemtheoretischen Literatur- und Kommunikationswissenschaft (Hallische Medienarbeiten) H. de Berg

Poets Laureate of the Holy Roman Empire *(Hungarian Journal of English and American Studies)* J. L. Flood

Gauvain's guilt in *L'Atre Perilleux*: the subtext of sexual abuse *(Reading Medieval Studies)* N. Thomas

W. Haug: *Vernacular literary theory in the Middle Ages: the German tradition, 800-1300, in its European context* (CUP) tr. J. M. Catling

Anachronie; Analepse; Dauer; Frequenz; Metalepse; Prolepse. In: *Metzler Lexikon Literatur- und Kulturtheorie*, ed. A. Nünning (Metzler) B. Müller

Analytical and textual bibliography in Germany and in Italy. In: *The book encompassed: studies in twentieth-century bibliography*, ed. P. Davison (St Paul's Bibliographies & Oak Knoll Press) J. L. Flood & C. Fahy

Streifzüge durch die englische Literatur (Insel) R. Görner

Mephisto in modern English guise. In: *Cousins at one remove...* R. F. M. Byrn

Unity and difference in European cultures (Durham Modern Languages series) ed. N. Thomas & F. Le Saux

Some old and new perspectives on European unity. In: *Unity and difference in European cultures...* N. Thomas

Psychoanalytical criticism: a reappraisal (Polity) E. E. Wright

Coming out of feminism (Blackwell) E. E. Wright, M. Merck & N. Segal

Bertolt Brecht and critical theory: Marxism, modernity and the 'Threepenny' lawsuit, 2nd edn. (Lang) S. Giles

Ballads into books: the legacies of Francis James Child, 2nd edn. (Lang) ed. T. Cheesman & S. Rieuwerts

A Romantic in Ratzeburg: Coleridge's debt to North German *Provinz*. In: *Cousins at one remove...* I. Cornils

Re-writing, re-cycling: Friedrich Dürrenmatt and *The Tragedy of King John*. In: *Cousins at one remove...* S. G. Donald

Ebner-Eschenbach und Turgenjew: eine Begegnung im Prosagedicht. In: *Des Mitleids tiefe Liebesfähigkeit: zum Werk der Marie von Ebner-Eschenbach*, ed. J. Strelka (Lang) A. Stillmark

Cosmic quaternities in the *Roman de Fauvel*. In: *Fauvel studies: allegory, chronicle, music and image in Paris, Bibliothèque Nationale de France, MS français 146* , ed. M. Bent & A. Wathey (OUP) N. F. Palmer

George Eliot and Goethe: an elective affinity (Rodopi) G. Röder-Bolton

Goethe, Ossian and *Werther*. In: *From Gaelic to Romantic: Ossianic translations...* F. J. Lamport

Luise Gottsched und Dorothea Tieck: vom Schicksal zweier Übersetzerinnen (*Shakespeare-Jahrbuch*) R. C. Paulin

'Je eigentümlicher das Original, desto schwieriger die Übersetzung.' The *Fairy Tales* of the Brothers Grimm in Irish translation. In: *Deutsch-irische Verbindungen...* A. McTigue

Who are we now? Christian humanism and the global market from Hegel to Heaney (University of Notre Dame Press & T. & T. Clark) N. Boyle

Judge Adam of Ballybog: two transpositions of Kleist's *Der zerbrochne Krug* to Irish contexts (*Translation Ireland*) T. E. Bourke

'Blast, rief Cuchullin ...!' Lenz and Ossian. In: *From Gaelic to Romantic: Ossianic translations...* H. Gaskill

Luhmann in literary studies: perspectives and problems. In: *Mutual exchanges...* H. de Berg

Marinetti: *Mafarka the Futurist* (Middlesex University Press) tr. C. Diethe

Ossian. In: *Goethe-Handbuch 4*, ed. B. Witte, T. Buck, H.-D. Dahnke, R. Otto & P. Schmidt (Metzler) H. Gaskill

Chemical solutions: scientific paradigms in Nietzsche and Proust. In: *The Third Culture: literature and science*, ed. E. Shaffer (de Gruyter) D. Large

Ellis Peters and Brother Cadfael and the medieval whodunnit (*Quaderni della Facoltà di Lingue e Letterature Straniere Moderne, Università degli Studi di Genova*) J. Margetts

Rilke als Übersetzer: Elizabeth Barrett-Browning's sonnets from the Portuguese. In: *Rilke: ein europäischer Dichter aus Prag*, ed. P. Demetz, J. W. Storck & H. D. Zimmermann (Königshausen & Neumann) J. M. Catling

Rilke jako překladatel: Portugalskych sonetů Elizabeth Barrett-Browningové. In: *Rainer Maria Rilke: Evropsky Básniík z Prahy. Sborník z mezinárodní konference* (H+H) J. M. Catling

Literaturnaya Ispoved: Josef Rot i Dostoyevskij (*Dostoyevskij i Mir Iskusstva Almanach*) A. Stillmark

Schiller, Kleist, Wagner: a great British tradition? In: *Cousins at one remove...* F. G. T. Bridgham

Tennyson's *Idylls* and Wagner's *Ring*: a case for cultural convergence of mythopoeic influence? In: *Myth and the making of modernity*, ed. M. Bell & P. Poellner (Rodopi) M. Oergel

Von der Utopie zur Anti-Utopie: über H. G. Wells *The Time Machine* (*Diagonal*) J. Schäfer

'überhaupt tendiert alles auf Fassen von Geschichte': Varianten der Geschichts-aneignung bei Virginia Woolf und Ingeborg Bachmann. In: *Fiktion und Geschichte in der anglo-amerikanischen Literatur,* ed. R. Ahrens & F. W. Neumann (Winter) S. Hotho

B 2 German literature: general studies (incl. specific themes and genres)

The Cambridge Companion to modern German culture (CUP) ed. E. Kolinsky & W. van der Will

Towards emancipation: German women writers of the 19th century (Berghahn) C. Diethe

In search of German culture. In: *The Cambridge Companion to modern German culture*... E. Kolinsky & W. van der Will

The Austrian comic tradition: studies in honour of W. E. Yates. Austrian Studies 9 (Edinburgh University Press) ed. J. R. P. McKenzie & L. Sharpe

The continuity of visual poetry: from a typology to a systematics. In: *A point of view: visual poetry in the 90s* (Dmitry Bulatov) J. D. Adler

Sinti and Roma: gypsies in German-speaking society and literature (Berghahn) ed. S. C. Tebbutt

Sinti and Roma: from scape-goats and stereotypes to self-assertion. In: *Sinti and Roma*... S. C. Tebbutt

Piecing together the jigsaw: the history of the Sinti and Roma in Germany. In: *Sinti and Roma*... S. C. Tebbutt

Challenging new literary images of Sinti and Roma. In: *Sinti and Roma*... S. C. Tebbutt

Conclusion. In: *Sinti and Roma*... S. C. Tebbutt

Germany. In: *Encyclopedia of the novel*, ed. P. E. Schellinger (Fitzroy Dearborn) M. E. Humble

Moritat. In: *Enzyklopädie des Märchens*, vol. 9, ed. R. W. Brednich *et al.* (de Gruyter) T. Cheesman

'Die Zung' ist dieses Schwert': classical tongues and gendered curricula in German schooling to 1908. In: *Pedagogy and power: rhetorics of classical learning*, ed. Y. L. Too & N. Livingstone (CUP) S. Colvin

The case for gender issues in German studies. In: *German studies: old and new challenges*... E. Boa

The case for specialist studies: Jewish studies. In: *German studies: old and new challenges*... F. Krobb

Kritik der Dialogizität: jenseits der Asymmetrien literarischer Kommunikation (*Lumis*) C. B. Grant

Modern German poetry. In: *The Cambridge Companion to modern German culture*... K. J. Leeder

Philologie als Hindernis: zur Negativität von Wissenschaft. In: *Akten des Frankfurter Germanistentreffens 1996* (Niemeyer) T. J. Reed

Freedom and pragmatism: aspects of religious toleration in eighteenth-century Germany (*Patterns of Prejudice*) R. N. N. Robertson

Marxist aesthetics and cultural modernity in *Der Dreigroschenprozeß*. In: *Bertolt Brecht: centenary essays*, ed. S. Giles & R. Livingstone (Rodopi) S. Giles

Bertolt Brecht and critical theory: Marxism, modernity and the 'Threepenny' lawsuit... S. Giles

Jakob Julius David. In: *Major figures of nineteenth-century Austrian literature*, ed. D. E. Daviau (Ariadne Press) F. Krobb

Who are we now? Christian humanism and the global market from Hegel to Heaney... N. Boyle

'In den dunkelsten Teil des weitläufigen Parkes.' Rococo gardens, *fin-de-siècle* epigonality and *Wahlverwandtschaften* echoes in Richard von Schaukal's novella *Eros* (*Modern Austrian Literature*) F. Krobb

B 3 German literature

B 3.1 To 1500

Autor und Autorschaft im Mittelalter: Kolloquium Meissen 1995 (Niemeyer) ed. E. Andersen, J. Haustein, A. Simon & P. Strohschneider

Offene Geheimnisse: versteckte und verdeckte Autorschaft im Mittelalter. In: *Autor und Autorschaft im Mittelalter*... J. L. Flood

Vernacular literary theory in the Middle Ages... tr. J. M. Catling

Minnesang zwischen Frauen- und Gottesdienst (*Germanic Notes and Reviews*) G. Rings

Women and hunting-birds are easy to tame: aristocratic masculinity and the early German love-lyric. In: *Masculinity in medieval Europe*, ed. D. Hadley & T. Skinner (Longman) M. G. Chinca

Wo Einhörner wandern: die Wahrnehmung der Fremde in Reiseberichten über das Heilige Land und Amerika. In: *Reisen, Entdecken, Utopien*, ed. A. Bhatti & H. Turk (Jahrbuch für Internationale Germanistik) A. Simon

The case for medieval studies. In: *German studies: old and new challenges*... W. H. Jackson

Visio Drycthelmi; Visio Fursei; Visio Lazari; Visio monachi Eyneshamensis; Visio Sancti Pauli [II]; Visiones Georgii. In: *Die deutsche Literatur des Mittelalters: Verfasserlexikon*, 10/2, ed. B. Wachinger (de Gruyter) N. F. Palmer

Authority and authenticity: comments on the prologues to the Old Frisian laws (*Amsterdamer Beiträge zur älteren Germanistik*) B. Murdoch

Zur Form und Funktion einiger Modelle der Autorenselbstdarstellung in der mittelalterlichen Heldenepik: *Wolfdietrich* und *Dietrichs Flucht*. In: *Autor und Autorschaft im Mittelalter*... S. Coxon

Zisterzienser und ihre Bücher: die mittelalterliche Bibliotheksgeschichte von Kloster Eberbach im Rheingau (Schnell & Steiner) N. F. Palmer

Eberbach (Nr. 27-31, 33). In: *Cîteaux 1098-1998: Rheinische Zisterzienser im Spiegel der Buchkunst*, ed. Landesmuseum Mainz (Reichert) N. F. Palmer

Accessus ad auctores: Autorkonzeptionen in mittelalterlichen Kommentartexten. In: *Autor und Autorschaft im Mittelalter*... A. M. V. Suerbaum

Autor und Autorschaft in der meisterlichen Liedkunst. In: *Autor und Autorschaft im Mittelalter*... A. M. Volfing

Sigmund Feyerabend's 'Das Reyßbuch deß heyligen Lands': a study in printing and literary history (Reichert) A. Simon

Gottfried's 'huote' excursus (*Tristan* 17817-18115) (*Medium Aevum*) A. M. Volfing

The Tristan illustrations in Ms London, BL Add. 11619, the 'Roman de Tristan en Prose' and the German Tristan Tapestries (*Tristania*) A. Deighton

Heinrich's confession in Hartmann's poem (*Mediaevistik*) D. Duckworth

'si enredete im niht vil mite': einige Bemerkungen zum *Erec* Hartmanns von Aue. In: *Der fremdgewordene Text: Festschrift für Helmut Brackert*, ed. S. Bovenschen, W. Frey, S. Fuchs, W. Raitz & D. Seitz (de Gruyter) J. Margetts

Siegfried's dragon fight in German literary tradition. In: *A Companion to the 'Nibelungenlied'*, ed. W. McConnell (Camden House) J. L. Flood

Politics in the *Nibelungenlied*. In: *A Companion to the 'Nibelungenlied'*... B. Murdoch

'Gen den sechzig jaren': observations on Oswald von Wolkenstein's use of numbers. In: *Festschrift für Anton Schwob*, ed. W. Hofmeister & B. Steinbauer (Universität Innsbruck) A. T. Robertshaw

Der spätmittelalterliche Autor als Herausgeber seiner Werke: Oswald von Wolkenstein und Hugo von Montfort. In: *Autor und Autorschaft im Mittelalter*... A. T. Robertshaw

Der Autor und seine Geliebte: zur fiktiven Autobiographie im *Ackermann aus Böhmen* des Johannes von Tepl. In: *Autor und Autorschaft im Mittelalter*... N. F. Palmer

Stand und Aufgabe der *Parzival*-Kommentierung: Bestandsaufnahme anläßlich des Erscheinens von Eberhard Nellmanns neuem *Parzival*-Kommentar (*Euphorion*) D. N. Yeandle

The ecumenical ideal in Wolfram von Eschenbach revisited (*Amsterdamer Beiträge zur älteren Germanistik*) N. Thomas

B 3.2 1500-1700

German studies: the sixteenth century (*YWMLS*) P. G. Macardle

The book in Reformation Germany. In: *The Reformation and the book*, ed. J.-F. Gilmont (Ashgate) J. L. Flood

Wo Einhörner wandern: die Wahrnehmung der Fremde in Reiseberichten über das Heilige Land und Amerika. In: *Reisen, Entdecken, Utopien...* A. Simon

Zum literarischen Leben Leipzigs in der Mitte des 17. Jahrhunderts. In: *Stadt und Literatur im deutschen Sprachraum der frühen Neuzeit*, ed. K. Garber, S. Anders & T. Elsmann (Niemeyer) A. J. Harper

Consolatory dialogue in devotional writings by men and women of early modern Protestant Germany (*MLR*) A. Carrdus

Das Schloß als Festort in der frühen Neuzeit. In: *Die Künste und das Schloß in der frühen Neuzeit*, ed. L. Unbehaun, V. Schütte, & A. Beyer (Deutscher Kunstverlag) H. Watanabe-O'Kelly

Entries, firework displays and religious festivals in the Empire. In: *Spectaculum europaeum...* H. Watanabe-O'Kelly

Tournaments in Europe. In: *Spectaculum europaeum...* H. Watanabe-O'Kelly

'Sonst bisher nicht erfasst': unrecorded texts from the German Baroque. An occasional series to supplement Dünnhaupt's 'Personalbibliographien zu den Drucken des Barock' (Cat's Whiskers Press) ed. W. A. Kelly

Sigmund Feyerabend's 'Das Reyßbuch deß heyligen Lands'... A. Simon

Grimmelshausen the storyteller (Camden House) A. Menhennet

'But is it art?' Polarities in Harsdörffer's storytelling (*Daphnis*) A. Menhennet

Siegfried's dragon fight in German literary tradition. In: *A Companion to the Nibelungenlied...* J. L. Flood

B 3.3 The eighteenth century and the Classical Age

The Classical era (*YWMLS*) D. Hill

Women writers in the Age of Goethe 10 (University of Lancaster) ed. M. C. Ives

'Römisches Carneval' und Weimarischer Maskenzug: Variationen zum Thema Chaos und Ordnung (*Internationales Archiv für Sozialgeschichte der Deutschen Literatur*) A. Köhler

Rhyme and reason: Enlightenment by other means. Presidential address to the English Goethe Society (*PEGS*) T. J. Reed

The discreet charm of the Belvedere: submerged homosexuality in eighteenth-century writing on art (*GLL*) J. Morrison

England. In: *Goethe-Handbuch 4...* H. B. Nisbet

Heroes in their underclothes: Aloys Blumauer's travesty of Virgil's *Aeneid*. In: *The Austrian comic tradition...* R. N. N. Robertson

Goethe. In: *Routledge encyclopedia of philosophy*, ed. E. Craig (Routledge) N. Boyle

Goethe, Schelling's theology and the genesis of *Prooemion* (*DVjs*) A. T. Fineron

The complete Goethe (*TLS*) J. D. Adler

Naturgeschichte und Humangeschichte bei Goethe, Herder und Kant. In: *Goethe und die Verzeitlichung der Natur*, ed. P. Matussek (Beck) H. B. Nisbet

'Werther's reading of Hirschfeld's *Landleben*: on the genesis of Werther's second letter. In: *London German Studies VI...* J. D. Adler

Introduction and notes. In: Goethe: *Maxims and reflections*, tr. E. Stopp (Penguin) P. Hutchinson

Introduction. In: Goethe: *Selected poems*, tr. J. Whaley (Dent) M. G. Bell

Goethe and the Hamiltons (*OGS*) D. J. Constantine

Goethe und die englische Literatur: Goethe und Carlyle. In: *Goethe-Handbuch 4...* T. J. Reed

Tag- und Nachtseiten des animalischen Magnetismus: zur Polarität von Wissenschaft und Dichtung bei Goethe. In: *Goethe und die Verzeitlichung der Natur...* J. Barkhoff

Luise Gottsched und Dorothea Tieck: vom Schicksal zweier Übersetzerinnen (*Shakespeare-Jahrbuch*) R. C. Paulin

Who are we now? Christian humanism and the global market from Hegel to Heaney... N. Boyle

Herder's conception of nationhood and its influence in eastern Europe. In: *The German lands and eastern Europe*, ed. R. Bartlett & K. Schönwälder (Macmillan) H. B. Nisbet

Hölderlin and the dynamics of translation (EHRC/BCLA) C. Louth

Hölderlin: poems and fragments, tr. M. Hamburger (Penguin) ed. J. D. Adler

Palastrevolution. Kant, Schiller und die Geburt einer Ästhetik aus dem Geist der Politik. In: *'In Spuren gehen...' Festschrift für Helmut Koopmann* (Niemeyer) T. J. Reed

Heinrich von Kleist: the ambiguity of art and the necessity of form (OUP) H. M. Brown

Über Kleists *Michael Kohlhaas*: Kohlhaas und Brandenburg. In: *Mutual exchanges...* R. J. Kavanagh

'Blast, rief Cuchullin ...!' Lenz and Ossian. In: *From Gaelic to Romantic: Ossianic translations...* H. Gaskill

Masonic thought in the work of Karl Philipp Moritz: sheen or substance? In: *London German Studies VI...* E. M. Batley

Ossian. In: *Goethe-Handbuch 4...* H. Gaskill

'Dies hohe Lied der Duldung'? The ambiguities of toleration in Lessing's *Die Juden* and *Nathan der Weise* (*MLR*) R. N. N. Robertson

Lessing. In: *Encyclopedia of aesthetics*, ed. M. Kelly (OUP) H. B. Nisbet

'Ó nach bocht an teanga an Ghaeilg! Cad é mar teanga tuatach!' A note on an Irish translation of Lessing's *Minna von Barnhelm*. In: *Deutsch-irische Verbindungen...* R. Ní Néill

Lukrez. In: *Goethe-Handbuch 4...* H. B. Nisbet

Friedrich Schiller. In: *Routledge encyclopedia of philosophy...* T. J. Reed

The revenge of the 'untere Seelenvermögen' in Schiller's dramas (*GLL*) M. G. Bell

From Samaritan to criminal: Schiller, Droste and the ballad. In: *Women writers in the Age of Goethe...* J. D. Guthrie

Schiller and the 'European Community': universal history in theory and practice (*MLR*) F. J. Lamport

Schiller: *Mary Stuart* (Penguin) ed. & tr. F. J. Lamport

Schiller, Leben und Persönlichkeit; Schiller und die Weimarer Klassik. In: *Schiller-Handbuch*, ed. H. Koopmann (Kröner) T. J. Reed

Zwischen Intertext und Steckenpferd: Überlegungen zum Erkenntnisproblem in *Tobias Knaut* (*Wezel-Jahrbuch*: *Studien zur deutschen Aufklärung*) D. Hill

B 3.4 The Romantic Age

The Romantic era (*YWMLS*) S. Dickson

Romantic dreams (University of Glasgow French and German Publications) ed. S. Dickson & M. G. Ward

Occasions (Austrian Cultural Institute) R. Görner

Experimentelle Selbsterfahrung und Selbstdestruktion: Anatomie des Ichs in der literarischen Moderne. In: *Ästhetische Moderne in Europa: Grundzüge und Problemzusammenhänge seit der Romantik*, ed. S. Vietta & D. Kemper (Fink) N. D. B. Saul

Making dreams come true in the works of Achim von Arnim. In: *Romantic dreams...* S. Dickson

Dreams and dreaming in the works of Joseph von Eichendorff. In: *Romantic dreams...* J. Purver

Freud and the Erl King (*OGS*) J. Simpson

Goethe and patriarchy: Faust and the fates of desire (Oxford / EHRC) J. Simpson

Luise Gottsched und Dorothea Tieck: vom Schicksal zweier Übersetzerinnen (*Shakespeare-Jahrbuch*) R. C. Paulin

Who are we now? Christian humanism and the global market from Hegel to Heaney... N. Boyle

Irrationalismus und jüdisches Schicksal: die thematischen Zusammenhänge von Heines *Ideen. Das Buch le Grand.* In: *Heinrich Heine: Aufklärung und Skepsis*, ed. J. Kruse, K. Füllner & B. Witte (Metzler) M. F. Perraudin

Heines Körperteile: zur Anatomie des Dichters. In: *Heine und die Weltliteratur: London Heine Conference 1997* (Oxford / EHRC) T. J. Reed

Unrequited dislike: Heine and England. In: *For freedom's battle: Heinrich Heine and England. A bicentenary exhibition* (Christie's) T. J. Reed

Karnevaleske Mesalliancen oder der Autor als Bauchredner der Sprache? Eine Analyse Bachtinscher Ansätze für die Interpretation des Traumes in Hoffmanns 'Die Abenteuer der Sylvester-Nacht' im Lichte der malerischen Intertexte. In: *Romantic dreams...* R. Schmidt

Der Dichter als Fledermaus bei der Schau des Wunderbaren: die Poetologie des rechten dichterischen Sehens in Hoffmanns 'Der Sandmann' und 'Das öde Haus'. In: *Mutual exchanges...* R. Schmidt

Some thoughts on affinities between Hugo and Büchner: a response to Thomas Bremer. In: *Vormärzliteratur in europäischer Perspektive II*, ed. M. Lauster, G. Oesterlo & S. Gröf (Aisthesis) J. Purver

Hot air over Berlin: Kleist, balloon flight and politics (*Colloquia Germanica*) J. Hibberd

Heinrich von Kleists report on Heligoland (*GLL*) J. Hibberd

Conrad Ferdinand Meyer: *Gedichte* (Insel) ed. R. Görner

Ludwig Tieck und die Musenalmanache und Taschenbücher. In: *Literarische Leitmedien*, ed. P. G. Klussmann *et al.* (Harrassowitz) R. C. Paulin

The comedies of Johanna von Weissenthurn. In: *The Austrian comic tradition...* I. F. Roe

B 3.5 1830-1890

Literature 1830-1880 (*YWMLS*) W. N. B. Mullan

The Biedermeier and beyond (Lang) ed. I. F. Roe & J. D. A. Warren

Attitudes towards nature in Biedermeier Vienna. In: *The Biedermeier and beyond...*
P. Branscombe

Jewish reflections on revolution. In: *Vormärzliteratur in europäischer Perspektive...*
A. M. Bunyan

Logis in einem Landhaus (Hanser) W. G. Sebald

Witiko and the absurd. In: *The Biedermeier and beyond...* H. Ragg-Kirkby

Wiener Wohnkultur. In: *The Biedermeier and beyond...* M. Rogers

Eduard von Bauernfeld and the beginnings of Austrian social drama. In: *The Biedermeier and beyond...* J. D. A. Warren

'Schade wär's / Auch um so manches herrliche Talent': Droste-Hülshoffs dramatische Versuche. In: *Women writers in the Age of Goethe...* S. Colvin

Als das Preußische verging: Fontane und Bismarck (*Neue Gesellschaft / Frankfurter Hefte*) R. Görner

Intertextualität als Zeitkommentar. Theodor Fontane, Gustav Freytag und Thomas Mann oder: Juden und Jesuiten. In: *Theodor Fontane und Thomas Mann*, ed. E. Heftrich *et al.* (Klostermann) E. Sagarra

'Nimm doch vorher eine Tasse Tee': Humor und Ironie bei Theodor Fontane und Thomas Mann. In: *Theodor Fontane und Thomas Mann...* M. Swales

Ludwig August Frankl and the reflection of the Biedermeier. In: *The Biedermeier and beyond...* C. Walker

Elizabeth Gaskell's German stories (*The Gaskell Society Journal*) P. N. Skrine

Die Jüdin von Toledo and changing views on women in the Biedermeier and beyond. In: *The Biedermeier and beyond...* I. F. Roe

Friedrich Halm and the comic muse. In: *The Austrian comic tradition...*
P. N. Skrine

The wandering court Jew and the hand of God: Jewish stereotypes and Wilhelm Hauff's *Jud Süß* (*MLR*) J. Chase

Who are we now? Christian humanism and the global market from Hegel to Heaney... N. Boyle

Riens de moins qu'une médiation: Heine et la peur de l'Angleterre (*Romantique*)
M. F. Perraudin

Heyse and Storm on the slippery slope: two differing approaches to euthanasia
(*GLL*) B. Burns

The short stories of Detlev von Liliencron: passion, penury, patriotism (Edwin Mellen) B. Burns

Eduard Mörike: 'Einer Reisenden'. Das Problem der Umkehr im Gedichtwerk. In: *Mutual exchanges...* F. A. Lösel

Nestroy: *Historisch-kritische Ausgabe: Stücke 17/II (Das Mädl aus der Vorstadt)* (Deuticke) ed. W. E. Yates

Nestroy: *Historisch-kritische Ausgabe: Stücke 26/II (Lady und Schneider* and *Judith und Holofernes)* (Deuticke) ed. J. R. P. McKenzie

Zur Entstehungs- und Überlieferungsgeschichte von Nestroys vorrevolutionären Possen *Zwey ewige Juden und Keiner* und *Der Schützling (Nestroyana)* J. R. P. McKenzie

Nestroy's *Zwey ewige Juden und Keiner*: a tale of three cities. In: *The Austrian comic tradition...* J. R. P. McKenzie

Nietzsche's Helmbrecht, or: How to philosophise with a ploughshare (*Journal of Nietzsche Studies*) D. Large

Friedrich Nietzsche: *Twilight of the Idols* (OUP) tr. & ed. D. Large

Journal of Nietzsche Studies (Nietzsche and German Literature) ed. D. Large

'Daß die Kunde nicht untergeht!' Pückler-Muskau and Freiligrath on the Irish tithe system. In: *Deutsch-irische Verbindungen...* T. E. Bourke

Wilhelm Raabe: *Meistererzählungen* (Manesse) ed. R. Görner

Any old iron? Some aspects of Raabe's realism in *Unruhige Gäste (Seminar)* W. P. Hanson

Having the last word, or, home truths from abroad: the reliable narrator in Wilhelm Raabe's *Unruhige Gäste (Neophilologus)* G. Opie

From Samaritan to criminal: Schiller, Droste and the ballad. In: *Women writers in the Age of Goethe...* J. D. Guthrie

Carl Schurz und seine Radikalisierung durch die Ereignisse von 1848 bis 1851. In: *Vormärzliteratur in europäischer Perspektive II...* T. E. Bourke

Ludwig Tieck und die Musenalmanache und Taschenbücher. In: *Literarische Leitmedien...* R. C. Paulin

Kaufmann und *homme de lettres à la fois*: Georg Weerth und die *Neue Rheinische Zeitung*. In: *Georg Weerth und das Feuilleton der 'Neuen Rheinischen Zeitung'*, ed. D. Kopp & M. Vogt (Aisthesis) U. Zemke

Historicizing Weininger: the nineteenth-century German image of the feminized Jew. In: *Modernity, culture and 'the Jew'*, ed. B. Cheyette & L. Marcus (Polity / Stanford University Press) R. N. N. Robertson

B 3.6 1890-1945

The Biedermeier and beyond... ed. I. F. Roe & J. D. A. Warren

The image of the Biedermeier age in early twentieth-century Vienna. In: *The Biedermeier and beyond...* W. E. Yates

Talking of modernity: the Viennese *Vortrag* as form (*GLL*) J. Stewart

Culture through literature through drama. In: *Foreign language learning in intercultural perspective: approaches through drama and ethnography*, ed. M. Byram & M. Fleming (CUP) M. L. Schewe

Modernism/Dada/Postmodernism (Northwestern University Press) R. Sheppard

The Unknown Soldier and the return of the fallen: the political dimension of mourning in German texts from the First World War to the present (*MLR*) M. E. Humble

'Keine Klage über England?' Deutsche und österreichische Exilerfahrungen in Großbritannien 1939-1945 (Iudicium / IGS) ed. C. Brinson, R. Dove, A. Grenville, M. Malet & J. Taylor

Die Kultur haben wir ihnen aufgehoben. Sie wurde nur nicht abgeholt. In: *'Keine Klage über England?'...* J. Taylor

Geschichte als Ausweg? Über den Aspekt der Historie in den Werken deutscher Exilautoren. In: *Vergangenheit vergegenwärtigen: der historische Roman im 20. Jahrhundert*, ed. M. Flothow & F. L. Kroll (Evangelische Verlagsanstalt) H. Siefken

Experimentelle Selbsterfahrung und Selbstdestruktion: Anatomie des Ichs in der literarischen Moderne. In: *Ästhetische Moderne in Europa...* N. D. B. Saul

An innocent abroad: the Pierrot figure in German and Austrian literature at the turn of the century (*PEGS*) R. Vilain

Logis in einem Landhaus... W. G. Sebald

Short journeys through inner space: metaphorical representations of mental events in some German *Novellen* from the 1890s to the 1930s (*FMLS*) D. Turner

Between cultures: German books in interwar Britain (*German Politics and Society*) E. Kolinsky

Exile studies in Great Britain. In: *Mutual exchanges...* J. M. Ritchie

Exiltheater in Großbritannien. In: *Handbuch des deutschsprachigen Exiltheaters 1933-1945*, vol. 1, *Verfolgung und Exil deutschsprachiger Theaterkünstler*, ed. F. Trapp, W. Mittenzwei, H. Rischbieter & H. Schneider (Saur) J. M. Ritchie

London-Gedichte von Exillyrikern in Großbritannien. In: *Deutschsprachige Exillyrik von 1933 bis zur Nachkriegszeit*, ed. J. Thunecke (Rodopi) J. M. Ritchie

Die Erneuerung des Judentums aus dem Geist der Assimilation, 1900 bis 1922. In: *Ästhetische und religiöse Erfahrungen der Jahrhundertwenden, Bd 2: um 1900*, ed. W. Braungart, G. Fuchs & M. Koch (Schöningh) R. N. N. Robertson

The 'body economic' in contemporary critiques of First World War propaganda (*FMLS*) G. Carr

Woman's rights or mother's duty? Feminist campaigns to improve women's education in the *Kaiserreich*. In: *Mutual exchanges...* C. Bland

The procreative male: male images of masculinity and femininity in right-wing German literature of the 1918-1945 period (*FMLS*) B. Niven

Im Telegrammstil der Seele: Peter Altenberg – eine Biographie (Böhlau) A. Barker

Rudolf Hans Bartsch's *Schwammerl* and the making of the Schubert myth. In: *The Biedermeier and beyond...* A. Stillmark

Walter Benjamin: intellectual, critic, visionary (*New Politics*) G. Bartram

'Mind the gap': reflections on the importance of allegory in Benjamin, Kafka and Brecht. In: *London German Studies VI...* M. Swales

Film und Psychoanalyse in Berlin 1925. In: *Materialien zu Leben und Werk Siegfried Bernfelds* (Strömfeld Nexus) K. Seerik & B. Eppensteiner

Blüte und Elend des Gedichts. Oder: Über das Poetische bei Brecht (*Schweizer Monatshefte*) R. Görner

The many faces of B. B. in fiction and memoir: from Fleisser and Feuchtwanger to Canetti and Weiss. In: *Bertolt Brecht: centenary essays...* J. Preece

Marxist aesthetics and cultural modernity in *Der Dreigroschenprozeß*. In: *Bertolt Brecht: centenary essays...* S. Giles

Bertolt Brecht and critical theory: Marxism, modernity and the 'Threepenny' lawsuit... S. Giles

Brecht and semiotics: semiotics and Brecht. In: *Bertolt Brecht: centenary essays...* J. J. White

Politisches Exil und poetische Verbannung in einigen Gedichten Bertolt Brechts. In: *Deutschsprachige Exillyrik...* T. Kuhn

Notions of collaboration. In: *Bertolt Brecht: centenary essays...* T. Kuhn

The suppressed science of society in *Leben des Galilei.* In: *Bertolt Brecht: centenary essays...* T. Holmes

Alfred Döblin. In: *Vergangenheit vergegenwärtigen...* H. Siefken

Alfred Döblin: *Berlin Alexanderplatz.* In: *Encyclopedia of the novel...* M. E. Humble

Tiefen der Zeit. Untiefen der Jahre. Heimito von Doderers 'österreichische Idee' und die 'Athener Rede'. In: *Exzentrische Einsätze*, ed. K. Luehrs (de Gruyter) A. Barker

Heimito von Doderer and Peter Altenberg: an Anglo-Saxon approach. In: *Exzentrische Einsätze*... A. Barker

Intertextualität als Zeitkommentar. Theodor Fontane, Gustav Freytag und Thomas Mann oder: Juden und Jesuiten. In: *Theodor Fontane und Thomas Mann*... E. Sagarra

'Nimm doch vorher eine Tasse Tee': Humor und Ironie bei Theodor Fontane und Thomas Mann. In: *Theodor Fontane und Thomas Mann*... M. Swales

Erich Fried. In: *Modern Germany: an encyclopedia of history, people, and culture, 1871-1990*, ed. D. K. Buse & J. C. Doerr (Garland) S. W. Lawrie

'Das große Turnierfeld, auf dem sie sich versuchen': Erich Fried's work for German radio (*GLL*) S. W. Lawrie

'Pro captu interpretis...': James A. Galston and the road to fame. In: *Anna Seghers in perspective*, ed. I. Wallace (Rodopi) G. P. Butler

Prinzipien der Hoffnung: Kindheitserlebnisse und Frauengestalten in den Romanen von Anna Gmeyner. In: *'Keine Klage über England?'*... E. Timms

Two sides of an anorexic coin in *Die Wahlverwandtschaften* and *Die Verwandlung*: Ottilie as *Heilige*, Gregor as *Mistkäfer* (*Orbis Litterarum*) S. Dickson

Totalitäre Erfahrung aus der Sicht eines christlichen Essayisten. Theodor Haecker in München. In: *Totalitäre Erfahrung*, ed. F. L. Kroll (Bouvier) H. Siefken

Gerhart Hauptmann and the Naturalist drama (Harwood) J. Osborne

Who are we now? Christian humanism and the global market from Hegel to Heaney... N. Boyle

Herzl's play *The New Ghetto* and the perplexities of assimilation. In: *From dream to reality: Herzl and 'Der Judenstaat'*, ed. R. Wistrich (Magnes) R. N. N. Robertson

Hermann Hesse: *Steppenwolf*. In: *Encyclopedia of the novel*... M. E. Stewart

Kurt Hiller: a 'Stänkerer' in exile 1933-1955 (*GLL*) J. M. Ritchie

Kurt Hiller: a 'Stänkerer' in exile 1933-1955. In: *The legacy of exile: lives, letters, literature*, ed. D. Vietor-Engländer (Blackwell) J. M. Ritchie

The aristocratic philanderer: reflections on Hofmannsthal's 'Der Schwierige'. In: *The Austrian comic tradition*... M. Swales

'Stop all the clocks'. Time and Times in the Vienna Operas of Hofmannsthal and Strauss. In: *The Austrian comic tradition*... R. Vilain

Was ist Subordination? Noch einmal Hofmannsthals *Reitergeschichte* (*Studia austriaca*) D. Turner

'Welttheater': Hofmannsthal, Richard von Kralik, and the revival of Catholic drama in Austria, 1890-1934 (MHRA / IGS) J. Beniston

Peter Huchel: a literary life in 20th-century Germany (Lang) S. Parker

Evasive Realism: narrative construction in Dostoevsky's and Janáček's *From the House of the Dead*. In: *Janaček Studies*, ed. P. Wingfield (CUP) R. Vilain & G. Chew

Kafka und das Christentum (*Der Deutschunterricht*) R. N. N. Robertson

Victor Klemperer (1881-1960): profile of a German writer. Reflections on his 'Third Reich' diaries (*GLL*) H. S. Reiss

Wolfgang Koeppen. In: *Modern Germany*... S. W. Lawrie

Elisabeth Langgässer. In: *Metzler Autorinnen Lexikon*, ed. R. Hof & I. Stephan (Metzler) C. Gelbin

Heinrich Mann (1871-1950). In: *Modern Germany*... B. Niven

Heinrich Mann and Arnold Zweig: Left-wing Nietzscheans? (*Journal of Nietzsche Studies*) M. E. Humble

Klaus Mann's novel *The Volcano*: a document of German emigration after 1933. In: *Exiles and migrants: crossing thresholds in European culture and society*, ed. A. Coulson (Sussex Academic Press) H. Rasche

Von Deutschland nach Europa: *Der Zauberberg* im europäischen Kontext. In: *Auf dem Weg zum Zauberberg*, ed. T. Sprecher (Thomas-Mann-Studien) T. J. Reed

Ein Nebenweg. In: *Begleittexte zum Reprint von Thomas Mann: Der Tod in Venedig* (Fischer) T. J. Reed

Thomas Manns Zeitdienst (*Thomas Mann Jahrbuch*) H. Siefken

Language and desire in Musil's *Törleß*. In: *London German Studies VI*... A. Kramer

Preface. In: *Robert Musil: diaries 1899-1942*, ed. M. Mirsky (Basic Books) J. P. Payne

In pursuit of a post-conventional morality: critical reflections of Nietzsche's thought in Musil's *Man without Qualities* (*Journal of Nietzsche Studies*) D. Midgley

Almost an English author: Robert Neumann's English-language novels (*GLL*) R. A. Dove

Marching on: Karl Otten at the BBC. In: *'Keine Klage über England?'*... R. A. Dove

Alfons Petzold – Stefan Zweig: Briefwechsel (Lang) ed. D. Turner

Remarque against war: essays for the centenary of E. M. Remarque 1998 (SPIGS) ed. B. Murdoch, M. Ward & M. Sargeant

Bäumer's diary. In: *Remarque against war...* B. Murdoch

The continued appeal of the western front. In: *Remarque against war...* B. Thompson

The conflict of education. In: *Remarque against war...* C. Martin

Pacifism, politics and art. In: *Remarque against war...* K. Norrie & M. Read

A lost war: *Zeit zu leben und Zeit zu sterben*. In: *Remarque against war...* M. Sargeant

The KZ experience: *Der Funke Leben* and recent work on the Holocaust in literature. In: *Remarque against war...* H. Valencia

Rilke als Übersetzer: Elizabeth Barrett-Browning's sonnets from the Portuguese. In: *Rilke – ein europäischer Dichter aus Prag...* J. M. Catling

Rilke jako překladatel: Portugalskych sonetů Elizabeth Barrett-Browningové. In: *Rainer Maria Rilke: Evropsky Básniŕk z Prahy...* J. M. Catling

'Liebe und geschätzte Freundin': Rilkes Briefwechsel mit E. de W. (= Elizabeth de Waal) (*Jahrbuch der deutschen Schillergesellschaft*) J. M. Catling

'Schlecht kommen wir beide dabei nicht weg!' Joseph Roth's satire on the Emperor Franz Josef in his novel *Radetzkymarsch* (*Neophilologus*) B. Thompson

Bloodshed in the Balkans: Robert Scheu, Karl Kraus and a question of satire. In: *The Austrian comic tradition...* G. Carr

Schoenberg and German poetry. In: *Schoenberg and words: the modernist years*, ed. R. Bermann & C. Cross (Garland) R. Vilain

Anna Seghers: the British dimension. In: *Anna Seghers in perspective...* I. Wallace

The earliest reception of the Holocaust: Ernst Sommer's *Revolte der Heiligen* (*GLL*) A. Grenville

August Stramm (*Expresionismus in Teatru si in Arte, Semmel Teatral*) J. D. Adler

The laughter of Karl Thomas: madness and politics in the first version of Ernst Toller's *Hoppla, wir leben!* (*MLR*) K. Leydecker

Looking back at the revolution: Ernst Toller's *Eine Jugend in Deutschland* and Remarque's *Der Weg zurück*. In: *Remarque against war...* J. Fotheringham

B 3.7 Post-1945

German literature: 1945 to the present day (*YWMLS*) O. Evans

Experimentelle Selbsterfahrung und Selbstdestruktion: Anatomie des Ichs in der literarischen Moderne. In: *Ästhetische Moderne in Europa*... N. D. B. Saul

'Whose story?' Continuities in contemporary German-language literature (Lang) ed. A. Williams, S. Parkes & J. Preece

German-language literature after the diversion. In: *'Whose story?'*... A. Williams

'The gender of thought': recollection, imagination, and eroticism in fictional conceptions of East and West German identity. In: *'Whose story?'*... R. Schmidt

Recasting historical women: female identity in German biographical fiction (Berg) S. Bird

What is a classic? Responses from contemporary Germany (*PEGS*) O. Durrani

Das persische Abendessen: ein Unterrichtsversuch zu Selbst- und Fremdverstehen (*Deutsch Unterricht*) G. Rings

How many cultures make a sub-culture? Turkish migrant literature in Germany. In: *Unity and difference in European cultures*... J. Tudor

'Other' Austrians: post-1945 Austrian women's writing (Lang) ed. A. L. Fiddler

Klösterreich: memories of a Catholic girlhood. In: *'Other' Austrians...* P. M. Bagley

Exile studies in Great Britain. In: *Mutual exchanges...* J. M. Ritchie

Exiltheater in Großbritannien. In: *Handbuch des deutschsprachigen Exiltheaters 1933-1945...* J. M. Ritchie

London-Gedichte von Exllyrikern in Großbritannien. In: *Deutschsprachige Exillyrik...* J. M. Ritchie

Following the scent: waymarkers in contemporary German-language literature (*GSLG Newsletter*) A. Williams

Literatur und Ökologie: zur Einführung. In: *Literatur und Ökologie,* ed. A. Goodbody (Rodopi) A. Goodbody

Radio plays. In: *Modern Germany...* M. Stone

Dialect, popular culture and national identity in Austria (*York Working Papers in Linguistics*) V. Martin

25 years of emancipation? Women in Switzerland 1971-1996 (Lang) ed. J. Charnley, M. J. Pender & A. Wilkin

Contemporary images of death and sickness: a theme in German-Swiss prose writing (Sheffield Academic Press) M. J. Pender

Ostdeutsche Literatur und DDR-Vergangenheit. In: *Wiedervereinigung Deutschlands: Festschrift zum 20jährigen Bestehen der Gesellschaft für Deutschlandforschung*, ed. K. Eckart, J. Hacker & S. Mampel (Duncker & Humblot) R. Woods

Prescribing for the new Germany: the journal *Frankfurter Hefte* in its first year of publication (1946) (*GLL*) A. Bushell

'Es geht nicht um Literatur.' Some observations on the 1990 *Literaturstreit* and its recent anti-intellectual implications (*GLL*) H.-J. Hahn

Interkulturelle Konfigurationen: zur deutschsprachigen Erzählliteratur von Autoren nichtdeutscher Herkunft (Iudicium) ed. M. Howard

'Die Schmerzen der endenden Art'. Ecological themes in the works of Sorbian writers from the 1970s to the 1990s. In: *Literatur und Ökologie...* P. Barker

Spree und Bosporus: 'Mutual exchanges' in einigen Europa-Bildern türkisch-deutscher AutorInnen. In: *Mutual exchanges...* M. McGowan

Central Europe: rebirth of an idea. In: *Unity and difference in European cultures...* F. Wefelmeyer

H. G. Adler: *Der Wahrheit verpflichtet. Interviews – Gedichte – Essays* (Bleicher) ed. J. D. Adler

H. G. Adler und seine Freunde: vermischte Erinnerungen (*Marbacher Magazin*) J. D. Adler

The sounds of silence: Ilse Aichinger's *Die größere Hoffnung, Der Gefesselte*, and *Kleist, Moos, Fasane*. In: *'Other' Austrians...* B. Haines

Stefan Andres: der christliche Humanist als Kritiker seiner Zeit (Lang) J. M. Klapper

'Dieses Spannungsverhältnis, an dem wir wachsen': utopian impulses at the level of narrative discourse in Ingeborg Bachmann's *Simultan* (*Sprachkunst*) V. O'Regan

Jurek Becker (University of Wales Press) ed. C. Riordan

'Wie ich ein Deutscher wurde': Sprachlosigkeit, Sprache und Identität bei Jurek Becker. In: *Jurek Becker...* D. Rock

'Ich bezweifle, ob ich je DDR-Schriftsteller gewesen bin': Gespräch mit Jurek Becker. In: *Jurek Becker...* P. O'Doherty & C. Riordan

German literature and its discontents: Jurek Becker's *Warnung vor dem Schriftsteller*. In: *Jurek Becker...* R. W. Williams

'Wir sind auch nur ein Volk': Jurek Becker's television series. In: *Jurek Becker...* M. McGowan.

Silvio Blatters Romantrilogie *Tage im Freiamt*: Der Öko-Roman zwischen Heinrich Böll und Adalbert Stifter. In: *Literatur und Ökologie...* J. H. Reid

Private and public filters: Heinrich Böll's war as remembered in his fiction and his non-fiction. In: *European memories of the Second World War*, ed. C. Burdett, C. Gorrara & H. Peitsch (Berghahn) J. H. Reid

Heinrich Böll und das Kulturerbe. In: *Heinrich Böll – Ein Werk überwindet Grenzen*, ed. A. Bernáth (Szeged / JATE) J. H. Reid

Heinrich Böll: 'Anekdote zur Senkung der Arbeitsmoral' und 'Du fährst zu oft nach Heidelberg'. In: *Vom Nullpunkt zur Wende: Interpretationen und Materialien*, ed. H. Krauss & R. Sommer (Klartext) W. T. Webster

'Ein Schriftsteller, der funktioniert, ist keiner mehr': Heinrich Böll and the *Gruppe 47 (German Monitor)* F. J. Finlay

Wie und warum... *(Jahreshefte der Internationalen Wolfgang-Borchert-Gesellschaft)* G. J. A. Burgess

Warum Borchert? *(Jahreshefte der Internationalen Wolfgang-Borchert-Gesellschaft)* G. M. Sharman

Brecht, SED cultural policy and the issue of authority in the arts: the struggle for control of the German Academy of Arts. In: *Bertolt Brecht: centenary essays...* P. Davies & S. Parker

Bertolt Brecht and Anna Seghers: utopian additions to the critique of the Gotha Programme. In: *Bertolt Brecht: centenary essays...* J. Thomaneck

Pop-Literatur: Rolf Dieter Brinkmann und das Verhältnis zur Populärkultur in der Literatur der sechziger Jahre (M & P) J. Schäfer

Die Mythen der Erde – Nevfel Cumarts Lyrik. In: *Nevfel Cumart: Waves of Time – Wellen der Zeit. Poems – Gedichte* (Grupello) T. E. Bourke

From monologue to dialogue: the case of Delius's *Die Birnen von Ribbeck*. In: *'Whose Story?'...* O. Durrani

Interkulturelle Ichkonfiguration: zu Renan Demirkans *Die Frau mit Bart* und Franco Biondis *Die Unversöhnlichen*. In: *Interkulturelle Konfigurationen...* M. Howard

Heimito von Doderer and Peter Altenberg: an Anglo-Saxon approach. In: *Exzentrische Einsätze...* A. Barker

Desire and complicity in Anne Duden's *Das Judasschaf (MLR)* S. Bird

Günther Eich. In: *Modern Germany...* M. Stone

Der Autor in der Medienindustrie: Hans Magnus Enzensberger und Alexander Kluge. In: *Baustelle Gegenwartsliteratur: Die neunziger Jahre*, ed. A. Erb (Westdeutscher Verlag) M. Uecker

Ota Filip. In: *Kritisches Lexikon zur deutschsprachigen Gegenwartsliteratur*, ed. H. L. Arnold (text + kritik) J. Jordan

Erich Fried. In: *Modern Germany...* S. W. Lawrie

'Das große Turnierfeld, auf dem sie sich versuchen': Erich Fried's work for German radio (*GLL*) S. W. Lawrie

Fate and the fool, or Biedermann's antagonies. In: *London German Studies VI...* R. Gillett

Fühmanns heimliche Odyssee: die Rezeption von James Joyce in seinem Werk. In: *Jeder hat seinen Fühmann: Zugänge zu Poetologie und Werk Franz Fühmanns*, ed. B. Krüger, M. Bircken & H. John (Lang) G. D. Tate

The spectre of the apocalypse in the work of Franz Fühmann. In: *Literatur und Ökologie...* G. D. Tate

'Pro captu interpretis...': James A. Galston and the road to fame. In: *Anna Seghers in perspective...* G. P. Butler

Oskar Maria Graf: the centenary of a Bavarian Balzac? In: *London German Studies VI...* J. Margetts

'Und gestern, da hörte uns Deutschland': NS-Autoren in der Bundesrepublik. Kontinuität und Diskontinuität bei Friedrich Griese, Werner Beumelburg, Eberhard Wolfgang Möller und Kurt Ziesel (Königshausen & Neumann) S. Busch

Elfin-rustling, air and ashes: communication, identity and war in Ludwig Harig's *Ordnung ist das ganze Leben*. In: *War and identity*, ed. T. Thornton & B. Taithe (Sutton) K. M. Howard

The cost of loving: love, desire and subjectivity in the work of Marlen Haushofer. In: *'Other' Austrians...* M. Littler

Who are we now? Christian humanism and the global market from Hegel to Heaney... N. Boyle

Christoph Hein (1944–). In: *Modern Germany...* B. Niven

A play about Socialism? The reception of Christoph Hein's *Die Ritter der Tafelrunde*. In: *'Whose story?'...* B. Niven

'Unverhofftes Wiedersehen': narrative paradigms in Christoph Hein's *Nachtfahrt und früher Morgen* and *Exekution eines Kalbes* (*GLL*) G. M. Jackman

Stefan Heym's Radek: the conscience of a revolutionary (*GLL*) M. Tait

The Stefan Heym archive. In: *Cambridge University Library: the great collections*, ed. P. Fox (CUP) P. Hutchinson

History as biography as fiction: Wolfgang Hildesheimer's *Marbot: eine Biographie*. In: *'Whose story?'...* J. Long

Kurt Hiller: a 'Stänkerer' in exile 1933-1955 (*GLL*) J. M. Ritchie

Kurt Hiller: a 'Stänkerer' in exile 1933-1955. In: *The legacy of exile: lives, letters, literature...* J. M. Ritchie

Tactical realisms: Hochhuth's *Wessis in Weimar* and Kroetz's *Ich bin das Volk*. In: *'Whose story?'* ... D. Barnett

Peter Huchel: a literary life in 20th-century Germany (Lang) S. Parker

Distorted reflections: the public and private faces of the author in the work of Uwe Johnson, Günter Grass and Martin Walser, 1965-1975 (Rodopi) S. Taberner

Helga Königsdorf: 'Bolero'; Angela Krauss: 'Entdeckungen bei fahrendem Zug'; Rainer Kunze: 'Sechzehn'; Maxie Wander: 'Gabi A., Schülerin. Die Welt mit Opas Augen'. In: *Vom Nullpunkt zur Wende. Interpretationen und Materialien* ... K. McPherson

Wolfgang Koeppen. In: *Modern Germany*... S. W. Lawrie

The elusive first person plural: real absences in Reiner Kunze, Bernd-Dieter Hüge, and W. G. Sebald. In: *'Whose story?'*... A. Williams

Elisabeth Langgässer. In: *Metzler Autorinnen Lexikon*... C. Gelbin

Siegfried Lenz. In: *Modern Germany*... G. J. A. Burgess

Heinrich Mann (1871-1950). In: *Modern Germany*... B. Niven

Inszenierungen des unendlichen Gesprächs: zu Friederike Mayröckers langer Prosa. In: *'Other' Austrians*... A. Kramer

Anna Mitgutsch: *Abschied von Jerusalem*. An Austrian writer's presentation of a divided city. In: *'Other' Austrians*... M. Stone

Erika Mitterer as a Christian writer: a study of the novel *Der Fürst der Welt* as a precursor of the later poetry. In: *'Other' Austrians*... M. C. Ives

vox populi, vox Austriae: dialect and identity in Felix Mitterer's dramas. In: *Post-war Austrian drama*, ed. F. Finlay & R. Juetter (Rodopi) V. Martin

'Und immer zügelloser wird die Lust' : constructions of sexuality in East German literatures. With special reference to Irmtraud Morgner and Gabriele Stötzer-Kachold (Lang) B. Linklater

'Unbeschreiblich köstlich wie die Liebe selber': food and sex in the work of Irmtraud Morgner (*MLR*) B. Linklater

Subjectivity (un)bound: Libuše Moníková and Herta Müller. In: *Germany and eastern Europe 1870-1996*, ed. K. Bullivant, G. Giles & W. Pape (de Gruyter) B. Haines

Herta Müller (University of Wales Press) ed. B. Haines

Herta Müller: Outline biography. In: *Herta Müller*... B. Haines

Metapher, Metonymie und Moral: Herta Müllers *Herztier*. In: *Herta Müller*... R. Schmidt

'Die Einzelheiten und das Ganze': Herta Müller and totalitarianism. In: *Herta Müller*... J. J. White

Gespräch mit Herta Müller. In: *Herta Müller*... B. Haines & M. Littler

Beyond alienation: the city in the work of Libuše Moníková and Herta Müller. In: *Herta Müller*... M. Littler

'Leben wir im Detail': Herta Müller's micro-politics of resistance. In: *Herta Müller*... B. Haines

Remembered things: the representation of memory and separation in *Der Mensch ist ein großer Fasan auf der Welt*. In: *Herta Müller*... D. Midgley

Bibliography 1991-1998. In: *Herta Müller*... O. Evans

Borderlines and communication: Sten Nadolny's *Die Entdeckung der Langsamkeit*. In: *'Whose story?'*... S. C. Tebbutt

Utopia, dystopia and realism in Christine Nöstlinger's children's books. In: *'Other' Austrians*... G. Steinke

Der Landvermesser auf der Suche nach der poetischen Heimat: Hanns-Josef Ortheils Romanzyklus (Heinz) H. Schmitz

Sprachenverkehr: hybrides Schreiben in Werken von Özdamar, Özakin und Demirkan. In: *Interkulturelle Konfigurationen*... E. Boa

Insanity, inspiration and insight: considering 'weibliche Denkweisen' in Elisabeth Reichart's *Sakkorausch*. In: *'Other' Austrians*... L. Ovenden

Representing abuse: Elisabeth Reichart's *La Valse* and Marlen Haushofer's *Wir töten Stella*. In: *'Other' Austrians*... J. Wigmore

Verlust und Verrat. Nachbemerkung zu Brigitte Reimann: *Die Geschwister* (Aufbau) K. McPherson

Narrative structure and the search for the self in Brigitte Reimann's *Franziska Linkerhand* (GLL) H. L. Jones

H. Rosendorfer: *Letters back to ancient China* (Dedalus) tr. M. Mitchell

Language and silence: Gerhard Roth's *Die Archive des Schweigens*. In: *'Whose story?'*... R. Halsall

About the possibility of a multicultural society: Hilde Spiel's *Die Früchte des Wohlstands* and *Mirko und Franca*. In: *'Other' Austrians*... A. Hammel

Austrian identity in a schizophrenic age: Hilde Spiel and the literary politics of exile and reintegration. In: *Austria 1945-95: fifty years of the Second Republic*, ed. K. R. Luther & P. Pulzer (Ashgate) E. Timms

Verena Stefan twenty years on: aesthetic and linguistic innovation in *Wortgetreu ich Träume* and *Es ist Reich Gewesen*. In: *'Whose story?'*... F. J. Rash

Marginalisation and memories: Ceija Stojka's autobiographical writing. In: *'Other' Austrians*... S. C. Tebbutt

'wenn die stimme im körper spricht und tanzt': Gabriele Stötzer-Kachold's writing the body. In: *'Whose story?'*... B. Linklater

Erotic provocations: Gabriele Stötzer-Kachold's reclaiming of the female body. In: *Women in German Yearbook* (University of Nebraska Press) B. Linklater

'Wie muß ein Satz aussehen, der Mut machen soll?' Zum Zusammenhang von Ökoengagement, Naturerfahrung und literarischer Form im Werk von Walter Vogt und Otto F. Walter. In: *Literatur und Ökologie*... J. Barkhoff

'Was Eigenes sagen': the many autobiographies of Peter Warwerzinek. In: *'Whose story?'*... J. Preece

Myth, memory, testimony, Jewishness: Grete Weil's *Meine Schwester Antigone*. In: *European memories*... M. McGowan

Relations of production? Christa Wolf's extended engagement with the legacy of Bertolt Brecht. In: *Bertolt Brecht: centenary essays*... R. Rechtien

Das ausgeschlossene Andere der abendländischen Zivilisation: zu Christa Wolfs *Medea*. In: *Literatur und Ökologie*... R. Schmidt

'Überhaupt tendiert alles auf Fassen von Geschichte': Varianten der Geschichtsaneignung bei Virginia Woolf und Ingeborg Bachmann. In: *Fiktion und Geschichte in der anglo-amerikanischen Literatur*... S. Hotho

B 4 Dutch literature

Pawns or prime movers? The Rhetoricians in the struggle for power in the Low Countries. In: *European medieval drama. Second International Conference on Aspects of European Medieval Drama, Camerino 4-6 July, 1997*, ed. S. Higgins (Università degli Studi di Camerino: Centro Linguistico di Ateneo) E. Strietman

Pawns or prime movers? The Rhetoricians in the struggle for power in the Low Countries (*European Medieval Drama*) E. Strietman

B 5 Scandinavian Literature

The final years: Hamsun and Nazi Germany. In: *Hamsun in Edinburgh. Papers read at the Conference in Edinburgh 1997*, ed. P. Graves & A. Kruse (Hamsun-Selskapet / Hamary) R. S. Furness

B 6 Yiddish literature

Ostjüdische Rezeption von Remarque. In: *E. M. Remarque – Leben, Werk und weltweite Wirkung*, ed. T. Schneider (Rasch) H. Valencia

C   HISTORY, SOCIETY, INSTITUTIONS

C 1 History, politics, sociology

C 1.1 To 1900

The Cambridge Companion to modern German culture... ed. E. Kolinsky & W. van der Will

'The redeeming Teuton': nineteenth-century notions of the Germanic in England and Germany. In: *Imagining nations*, ed. G. Cubitt (Manchester University Press) M. Oergel

Degeneration and Zionism: Max Nordau, the forgotten architect of Israel (*Jewish Quarterly*) L. Löb

Pfälzer in Irland: deutschstämmige Siedlungen in der Grafschaft Limerick. In: *Deutsch-irische Verbindungen...* H. Rasche

'Poor green Erin': German perspectives of the Irish Question in the mid-19th century. In: *The legacy of colonialism: gender and cultural identity in post-colonial societies*, ed. M. Ní Fhlathúin (Galway University Press) T. E. Bourke

Images of dominance and submission in German-Sorbian cultural relations. In: *Cultural negotiations: Sichtweisen des Anderen*, ed. T. Seidel & C. Brown (Francke) P. Barker

Benign authority and its cultivation in the Biedermeier. In: *The Biedermeier and beyond...* E. Sagarra

Non-German minorities, women and the emergence of civil society. In: *The Cambridge Companion to modern German culture...* E. Kolinsky

'Römisches Carneval' und Weimarischer Maskenzug: Variationen zum Thema Chaos und Ordnung (*Internationales Archiv für Sozialgeschichte der Deutschen Literatur*) A. Köhler

Historicism. In: *Routledge encyclopedia of philosophy...* C. J. Thornhill

Der zweite punische Krieg zwischen Fiktion und Realität (*Geschichte der Geschichtsschreibung*) G. Rings

Voies postales en Europe 1492-1700 (*Pour la Science*) P. Ries

Jewish reflections on revolution. In: *Vormärzliteratur in europäischer Perspektive II...* A. M. Bunyan

'Wir zweifeln nicht an dem endlichen Sieg der Wahrheit und des Rechts': the emancipation debate in *Der Israelit des neunzehnten Jahrhunderts* 1839-1845. In: *The German-Jewish dilemma...* A. M. Bunyan

Tysklands Historia (*Historiska Media*) M. J. A. Fulbrook

Josephine Butler's campaign against the double moral standard, and its repercussions in Germany. In: *Cousins at one remove*... I. Sharp

Who are we now? Christian humanism and the global market from Hegel to Heaney... N. Boyle

C 1.2 From 1900

Germanistik an Hochschulen in Großbritannien und Irland. Verzeichnis der Hochschullehrerinnen und Hochschullehrer. Germanists in Great Britain and Ireland. Directory of University Teachers of German 1997/98 (DAAD) J. L. Flood & S. A. Macke-Monteiro

The Cambridge Companion to modern German culture... ed. E. Kolinsky & W. van der Will

In search of German culture. In: *The Cambridge Companion to modern German culture*... E. Kolinsky & W. van der Will

25 years of emancipation? Women in Switzerland 1971-1996... ed J. Charnley, M. J. Pender & A. Wilkin

Im Vorfeld des Massenmords: Germanistik im Zweiten Weltkrieg. Eine Übersicht. (Gesellschaft für interdisziplinäre Forschung) G. Simon & J. Lerchenmüller

Politik der Vernichtung (Piper) P. Longerich

Emigré Germanists and the University of London. In: *'Keine Klage über England?'*... J. L. Flood

A woman's place...? German-speaking women in exile in Britain, 1933-1945 (*GLL*) C. Brinson

The Federal Republic of Germany. In: *Modern Germany*... M. J. A. Fulbrook

Talking of modernity: the Viennese *Vortrag* as form (*GLL*) J. Stewart

German *ab initio*: the German Department as a mere language school? In: *German studies: old and new challenges*... P. Wend

Sprache und Nation im deutschsprachigen Raum aus der Sicht der englischsprachigen Wissenschaft. In: *Sprache und bürgerliche Nation*... S. Barbour

Non-German minorities, women and the emergence of civil society. In: *The Cambridge Companion to modern German culture*... E. Kolinsky

Die NS-'Vergangenheitsbewältigung' in der DDR und ihre Widerspiegelung im narrativen Prozess (*Menora. Jahrbuch für deutsch-jüdische Geschichte*) C. Gelbin

Archiv der Erinnerung: Interviews mit Überlebenden der Shoah. Videographierte Lebenserzählungen und ihre Interpretationen (Verlag für Berlin-Brandenburg) ed. C. Gelbin, E. Lezzi, G. Hartman & J. Schoeps

Projektvorstellung und Einleitung. In: *Archiv der Erinnerung...* C. Gelbin &
E. Lezzi

Zwischen Anpassung und Verfolgung: die Lebensgeschichte eines ehemaligen
'jüdischen Mischlings'. In: *Archiv der Erinnerung...* C. Gelbin

Degeneration and Zionism: Max Nordau, the forgotten architect of Israel (*Jewish
Quarterly*) L. Löb

Die Stimme des Gewissens: der Widerstand der Studenten der Weißen Rose. In:
Mutual exchanges... H. Siefken

Strukturen rechten Denkens in Geschichte und Gegenwart: konservative Revolution
und Neue Rechte (*Mitteilungen des Instituts für Wissenschaft und Kunst*)
R. Woods

Settling accounts with history: Germany's difficulties in dealing with political crime
committed in the German Democratic Republic (*Svensk Juristtidning*) G. Shaw

La formation professionnelle. De l'Est à l'Ouest de l'Europe: comment réussir le
changement? (*Revue Internationale de l'Education*) G. Shaw & D. Parkes

La formation professionnelle. De l'Est à l'Ouest de l'Europe: comment réussir le
changement? (*Administration et éducation*) G. Shaw & D. Parkes

German education and society, from 1810 to the present (Berg) H.-J. Hahn

*The correspondence of Myles Dillon 1922-1925: Irish-German relations and Celtic
studies* (Four Courts Press) J. Fischer & J. Dillon

*'Keltischer Sprengstoff : eine wissenschaftsgeschichtliche Studie über die deutsche
Keltologie, 1900-1945* (Niemeyer) J. Lerchenmüller

German studies: old and new challenges... ed. P. R. Lutzeier

Work placement in a German-speaking country. In: *German studies: old and new
challenges...* J. Taylor

New media in German studies. In: *German studies: old and new challenges...*
H. Briel

Social authoritarianism and the Left: a case study of the PDS. In: *Mutual
exchanges...* P. Thompson

*The Party of Democratic Socialism in Germany: modern post-communism or
nostalgic populism?* (Rodopi) ed. P. Barker

From SED to PDS: continuity or renewal? In: *The Party of Democratic Socialism in
Germany...* P. Barker

Die Stellung der PDS im ostdeutschen Parteiensystem. In: *The Party of Democratic
Socialism in Germany...* O. Niedermayer

Searching for voters: PDS mobilisation strategies, 1994-97. In: *The Party of
Democratic Socialism in Germany...* H. Krisch

Die PDS in Rostock: eine Lokalstudie über die Anatomie einer postkommunistischen Partei. In: *The Party of Democratic Socialism in Germany*... L. Probst

The PDS in the political culture of Erfurt. In: *The Party of Democratic Socialism in Germany*... N. Hubble

Why does the PDS reach the parts that *Bündnis 90 / Die Grünen* cannot? In: *The Party of Democratic Socialism in Germany*... B. Harper

Die PDS zwischen Ideologie und politischer Realität. In: *The Party of Democratic Socialism in Germany*... D. Klein

Transnationale Vergleiche: Partei des Demokratischen Sozialismus, Parti Communiste Français, Partito della Rifondazione Comunista. Politische, ideologische und strategische Konvergenzen. In: *The Party of Democratic Socialism in Germany*... P. Moreau

Four-Way Street: the PDS vis-à-vis former communist parties of eastern Europe. In: *The Party of Democratic Socialism in Germany*... J. Bastian

Die SPD und die PDS. In: *The Party of Democratic Socialism in Germany*... K.-J. Scherer

Die Auseinandersetzungen von Bündnis 90 / Die Grünen mit der PDS. In: *The Party of Democratic Socialism in Germany*... E. Schroedter

The PDS and the strategic dilemmas of the German Left. In: *The Party of Democratic Socialism in Germany*... G. Minnerup

Das 'Zusammenwachsen' Deutschlands im Bereich des Bildungswesens: Perspektiven und Probleme aus englischer Sicht. In: *Festschrift für Oskar Anweiler zum 70. Geburtstag*   D. Phillips

Chancengleichheit in Deutschland. In: *Thematisch* (Thornes) G. Loftus

Structural change, political re-alignment and shifting identities: the emergence of Wales and Saxony as modern regions in Europe. In: *Regional Cultures*, ed. F. Engelstad *et al.* (JAI Press) J. Mathias

Die regionale Frage in Großbritannien: das Beispiel Wales. In: *Regionen in der Europäischen Union*, ed. R. Krämer (Berliner Debatte Wissenschaftsverlag) J. Mathias & J. Loughlin

Mobilisation régionale et échange politique aux Pays de Galles et dans les West Midlands. In: *Que gouvernent les régions de l'Europe*, ed. B. Jouve & E. Negrier (L'Harmattan) J. Mathias, J. Loughlin & A. Reilly

Europäisierung und regionale Mobilisierung in Wales und Katalonien: eine vergleichende Analyse. In: *Interaktive Politik in Europa: Regionen im Netzwerk der Integration*, ed. B. Kohler Koch *et al.* (Leske & Budrich) J. Mathias *et al.*

Wales in Europe: Welsh regional actors and European integration (University of Wales Press) J. Mathias & J. Loughlin

Mobilisations et coopérations régionales au Royaume-Uni. In: *Les territoires du neo-régionalisme*, ed. R. Balme (Economica) J. Mathias & J. Loughlin

Die regionale Frage im Vereinigten Königreich (*WeltTrends*) J. Mathias & J. Loughlin

Documentation report: 'Wales in Europe' and 'Regional policy' (*Regional & Federal Studies*) J. Mathias

Eigenart vs. *das Eigene*: German intellectuals in search of a concept of nationhood and national identity after unification (*Debatte*) H. Schmitz

Tysklands Historia (*Historiska Media*) M. J. A. Fulbrook

Dividing the past, defining the present: historians and national identity in the two Germanies. In: *Writing national histories: western Europe since 1800*, ed. S. Berger *et al.* (Routledge) M. J. A. Fulbrook

Violence. In: *Modern Germany...* D. Haselbach

Political terrorism, FRG (1945-1990). In: *Modern Germany...* F. Krause

The social construction of identity: theoretical perspectives. In: *A chorus of different voices: German-Canadian identities*, ed. A. Sauer & M. Zimmer (Lang) D. Haselbach

Social cohesion and transition dynamics. In: *Welfare states in transition: east and west*, ed. I. Collier *et al.* (Macmillan) J. Hölscher

Multiculturalism in a world of leaking boundaries (Lit-Verlag) ed. D. Haselbach

Identität, Authentizität und Anerkennung: Falltüren im Multikulturalismus-Diskurs (*Vorgänge*) D. Haselbach

Multiculturalism in the making? (*German Politics*) E. Kolinsky

Recasting East Germany (*German Politics*) C. Flockton & E. Kolinsky

Recasting East Germany: social transformation after the GDR (Cass) ed. C. Flockton & E. Kolinsky

Recasting East Germany: an introduction. In: *Recasting East Germany...* C. Flockton & E. Kolinsky

Multiculturalism in the making? Non-German minorities in the new *Länder*. In: *Recasting East Germany...* E. Kolinsky

Women, work and the family. In: *Recasting East Germany...* E. Kolinsky

Schmittian Economic Liberalism: post-war West Germany's 'Social Market Economy'. In: *Memory, history and critique: European identity at the millennium. Proceedings of the Fifth Conference of the International Society for the Study of European Ideas 1996* (University for Humanist Studies) D. Haselbach

Verfahrensrechtliche Kontrolle unfairer AGB in Großbritannien (*Recht der internationalen Wirtschaft*) C. P. Sobich

The 'German model' in decline. In: *East Germany's economic development: domestic and global aspects*, ed. J. Hölscher & A. Hochberg (Macmillan) J. Hölscher & J. Stephan

DDR-Geschichtswissenschaft und Geschichtspolitik. In: *Die DDR-Geschichtswissenschaft als Forschungsproblem (Historische Zeitschrift, Sonderdruck)*, ed. G. Iggers, K. Jarausch & M. Sabrow (Oldenbourg) M. J. A. Fulbrook

Debate: theoretical perspectives on the German Democratic Republic (*Bulletin of the German Historical Institute London*) M. J. A. Fulbrook

Keynes and Hayek: some remarks on capital. In: *Hayek – the economist and social philosopher: a critical retrospective*, ed. S. Frowen (Macmillan) J. Hölscher

Collective bargaining under the strain of unification (*European Industrial Review*) S. French

Social transformation and the family in post-communist Germany (Macmillan) ed. E. Kolinsky

Social transformation: issues and developments. In: *Social transformation and the family in post-communist Germany...* E. Kolinsky

Recasting biographies. In: *Social transformation and the family in post-communist Germany...* E. Kolinsky

The family transformed: structures, experiences, prospects. In: *Social transformation and the family in post-communist Germany...* E. Kolinsky

Women in Germany. In: *Women and politics in post-communist Europe*, ed. M. Rueschemeyer (Sharpe) E. Kolinsky

Women, work and the family in East Germany (*German Politics*) E. Kolinsky

In search of a future: Leipzig since the *Wende* (*German Politics and Society*) E. Kolinsky

Multilateralni politika Nemecka vuci zemin SE. In: *Vztahy SRN ke statum stredni Europy*, ed. V. Handl, J. Hon & O. Pick (Ustav mezinarodnich vztahu) V. Handl

SRN a rozsireni EU a NATO po Amsterdamu a Madridu. In: *Vztahy SRN ke statum stredni Europy...* V. Handl

Nemecko a Pobalsky Region. In: *Vztahy SRN ke statum stredni Europy...* A. Hyde-Price

Nemecke spolkove zeme a rozsirovani EU: mezi bezproblemovosti a problemovymi navaznostmi. In: *Vztahy SRN ke statum stredni Europy...* S. Collins & C. Jeffery

'Chalk and cheese'? British and German policy divergences with regard to the eastern enlargement of the European Union (*The Polish Quarterly of International Affairs*) S. Collins

The German *Länder* and EU eastern enlargement: between apple pie and issue linkage (*German Politics*) S. Collins & C. Jeffery

Les *Länder* allemands et l'Europe. In: *Que gouvernent les régions d'Europe?...* C. Jeffery

Deutschlands europäische Diplomatie: die Entwicklung des regionalen Milieus. In: *Effektivierung deutscher Europapolitik*, ed. W. Weidenfeld (Europa Union Verlag) W. E. Paterson, S. Bulmer & C. Jeffery

Germany and EMU. In: *Break out, break down or break in? Germany and the European Union after Amsterdam*, ed. W. E. Paterson & C. Lankowski (AICGS) W. E. Paterson

Exchange rate policy, fiscal austerity and integration: the Hungarian example. In: *Macroeconomic problems of EU enlargement to the east*, ed. H. Gabrisch (Macmillan) J. Hölscher

Formation of economic order in Central Europe: a note on German neoliberalism. In: *Politics and economics of Eastern Europe*, ed. F. Columbus (Nova Science) J. Hölscher

Britain and the changing European security system. In: *Bezpieczenstwo Panstw Europy. Koncepcie i Problemy Lat 90*, ed. B. Lominsky (Wydnawnictwo Uniwersytetu Slaskiego) A. Hyde-Price

NATO and European security: dilemmas and prospects. In: *Der Aufbau einer europäischen Sicherheitsarchitektur. Loccumer Protokoll*, ed. J. Calließ (Kirchliche Verwaltungsstelle) A. Hyde-Price

Organisation for Security and Cooperation in Europe. In: *The Annual Register*, ed. A. Day (Keesing's Worldwide) A. Hyde-Price

The OSCE and European security. In: *Rethinking security in post-Cold War Europe*, ed. W. Park & G. Wyn Rees (Longman) A. Hyde-Price

Patterns of international politics. In: *Developments in central and eastern European politics 2*, ed. J. Batt *et al.* (Macmillan) A. Hyde-Price

Electoral reform: learning from Germany (*Political Quarterly*) C. Jeffery

Approaching devolution in the UK: lessons from Germany? In: *Federalism: choices in law, institutions and policy*, ed. K. Malfliet & L. Nasyrova (Garant / Institute for European Policy) C. Jeffery

Isaiah Berlin. In: *Routledge dictionary of twentieth-century political thinkers*, 2nd edn., ed. R. Benewick & P. Green (Routledge) R. N. Hausheer

Willy Brandt: a political biography (Macmillan) B. Marshall

'The struggle continues': Rudi Dutschke's Long March. In: *Student protest: the sixties and after*, ed. G. J. De Groot (Longman) I. Cornils

'A great and benevolent friend': Letters from an exile to George Peabody Gooch (*europäische ideen*) C. Brinson & M. Malet

Paradoxos de intersubjetividade: teorias de interação em Habermas e Luhmann (*Princípios. Revista de Filosofia*) C. B. Grant

Special Issue: Habermas (*Forum Deutsch*) ed. C. B. Grant & G. Otte

Who are we now? Christian humanism and the global market from Hegel to Heaney... N. Boyle

Ruth Heinrichsdorff: an SAP activist in British exile. In: *'Keine Klage über England?'...* C. Brinson

Rudolf Hilferding and Europe's New Labour (*The European Legacy*) J. Thomaneck

Sir Joseph Jonas, university benefactor, Lord Mayor of Sheffield. German spy? Hidden Jew? In: *Mutual exchanges...* G. Newton

Helmut Kohl, 'The vision thing' and escaping the semi-sovereignty trap. In: *The Kohl Chancellorship*, ed. W. E. Paterson & C. Clemens (Cass) W. E. Paterson

Helmut Kohl. In: *Encyclopaedia of the European Union*, ed. D. Dinan (Macmillan) W. E. Paterson

Beyond Dachau: Irmgard Litten in England. In: *'Keine Klage über England?'...* M. Malet

Friedrich Meinecke. In: *Routledge encyclopaedia of philosophy...* R. N. Hausheer

Politische Verfolgung in der Weimarer Republik: der Fall des Medizinprofessors Georg Friedrich Nicolai (Lewinstein) an der Friedrich-Wilhelm-Universität Berlin 1919-1922. In: *Der Exodus aus Nazideutschland und die Folgen*, ed. C. Hassler & J. Wertheimer (Niemeyer) J. Lerchenmüller

Franz Oppenheimer's contribution to the theory of co-operation (*Communal Societies*) D. Haselbach

Maskenwechsel: wie der SS-Hauptsturmführer Schneider zum BRD-Hochschulrektor Schwerte wurde und andere Geschichten über die Wendigkeit deutscher Wissenschaft im zwanzigsten Jahrhundert (Gesellschaft für interdisziplinäre Forschung) G. Simon & J. Lerchenmüller

Dialectics, intersubjectivity and the openness to change: Michael Theunissen's negative theology of time (*Radical philosophy*) C. J. Thornhill

The Gestapo and the German political exiles in Britain during the 1930s: the case of Hans Wesemann – and others (*GLL*) C. Brinson

C 2 Business and management studies since 1900

Student mobility in the European Union as a means of developing cross-cultural capabilities. In: *Multicultural education: reflection on theory and practice*, ed. K. Häkkinen (University of Jyväskylä) U. Zemke

Vom Berufspraktikum in den Beruf. In: *Wirtschaftsdeutsch...* U. Zemke

Verhandeln gehört zum Geschäft: die Rolle des Dolmetschens bei der Ausbildung im Bereich 'Business German'. In: *Wirtschaftsdeutsch...* A. Riddell

Methodologische Überlegungen bei der Herstellung von Materialien für den Klassenunterricht. In: *Wirtschaftsdeutsch...* M. Howarth

Wirtschaftsdeutsch: mit Rollenspielen lehren und lernen. In: *Wirtschaftsdeutsch...* A. Jamieson

Irish-German business negotiations (*German-Irish Business News*) G. Martin

An interdisciplinary and cross-cultural approach to research: the GLOBE Project. In: *Proceedings of the 5th European Congress of Psychology*, ed. S. Cromie *et al.* (Psychological Association of Ireland) G. Martin *et al.*

Ethical theory in German business ethics research (*Journal of Business Ethics*) L. Preuss

On ethical theory in auditing (*Managerial Auditing Journal*) L. Preuss

La coopération franco-allemande dans les domaines de pointe (*DOCUMENTS – Revue des Questions Allemandes*) J.-M. Trouille

C 3 The press, the media, the arts

The book in Reformation Germany. In: *The Reformation and the book...* J. L. Flood

'Wir zweifeln nicht an dem endlichen Sieg der Wahrheit und des Rechts': the emancipation debate in *Der Israelit des neunzehnten Jahrhunderts* 1839-1845. In: *The German-Jewish dilemma...* A. M. Bunyan

Language learning in the age of satellite television (OUP) U. H. Meinhof

'Often sublime and always pathetic': settings of Scottish texts in Biedermeier Vienna and beyond. In: *The Biedermeier and beyond...* A. Barker

Sprachinseln: jiddische Publizistik in Wilna, London und Berlin, 1880-1930 (Böhlau) S. Marten-Finnis & H. Valencia

What does 'culture' mean in German cultural studies? In: *German studies: old and new challenges...* J. Sandford

A short history of the press and media in Sorbian (*Mercator Media Forum*) P. Barker

Prescribing for the new Germany: the journal *Frankfurter Hefte* in its first year of publication (1946) (*GLL*) A. Bushell

Polyglot politics: hip hop in Germany (*Debatte*) T. Cheesman

Multiculturalism, migration and racism: the role of the media: a comparative study of Australian and German print media (*Journal for Intercultural Studies*) N. McLelland & S. Luchtenberg

Fremdenfeindlichkeit und Fußball in Großbritannien. In: *Medien und Fremdenfeindlichkeit,* ed. B. Scheffer (Leske & Budrich) S. Lamb

The centenary of the Henry Simon Chair of German at Manchester (*GLL*) E. Sagarra

Die charmante Dame im Spiegel: zu dem Lied Hob. XXXIc: 17 (*Haydn-Studien*) D. McCulloch

Jugend in den fünfziger Jahren: Berlin – Ecke Schönhauser (Jugendbilder in den DDR-Medien. Medienberatung Nr. 6) H. Claus

Eine Kriminalkomödie mit Tiefgang: Der Bruch (Kriminalität in den DDR-Medien. Medienberatung Nr. 7) H. Claus

Varieté – Operette – Film: Berührungspunkte und Konkurrenzkampf aus der Sicht des Fachblatts *Der Artist*. In: *MusikSpektakelFilm: Musiktheater und Tanzkultur im deutschen Film 1922-1937*, ed. K. Uhlenbrok (text + kritik) H. Claus

Learning and teaching culture from an aesthetic perspective. In: *Intercultural communication and language learning...* M. L. Schewe

Europäische Kinokunst im Zeitalter des Fernsehens (Fink) ed. V. Roloff, H. Schanze & D. Scheunemann

Kinoästhetik – Fernsehästhetik: vom Wandel des Kinofilms unter dem Eindruck des Fernsehens. In: *Europäische Kinokunst im Zeitalter des Fernsehens...* D. Scheunemann

Multimedia: eine Herausforderung des Fremdsprachenunterrichts, 2nd. edn., ed. M. Löschmann (Lang) M. Hahn, S. Künzel & G. Wazel

Models or misfits? The role of screen heroines in GDR cinema. In: *Triangulated visions: women in recent German cinema*, ed. I. Majer O'Sickey & I. von Zadow (State University of New York Press) A. Rinke

Videotechnik und die Suche nach dem wahrhaftigen Bild: zur Zusammenarbeit Antonionis und Wenders'. In: *Europäische Kinokunst im Zeitalter des Fernsehens...* A. Graf

'It is in the inner realm that all dramas take place.' Afterword. In: Ingeborg Bachmann: *The radio plays*, tr. L. Friedberg (Ariadne) S. Colvin

Film und Psychoanalyse in Berlin 1925. In: *Materialien zu Leben und Werk Siegfried Bernfelds* (Strömfeld Nexus) K. Seerik & B. Eppensteiner

Bertolt Brecht and critical theory: Marxism, modernity and the 'Threepenny' lawsuit... S. Giles

Representing vulnerability: boundaries of race, gender, age and class in Rainer Werner Fassbinder's film *Fear Eats the Soul*. In: *In/visibility: gender and representation in a European context. Interface: Bradford studies in language, culture and society*, ed. R. M. Cleminson & M. E. Allison (University of Bradford) S. C. Tebbutt

Theater – Kino – Fernsehen: Formen der Intermedialität in Filmen Rainer Werner Fassbinders. In: *Europäische Kinokunst im Zeitalter des Fernsehens...* U. Militz

'Für Kultur ist es nie zu spät': Alexander Kluge's television programmes. In: *'Whose story?'...* M. Uecker

Happy Endings im Fernsehzeitalter: über Operndramatik und Kinoverständnis in Alexander Kluges *Die Macht der Gefühle* und Werner Herzogs *Fitzcarraldo*. In: *Europäische Kinokunst im Zeitalter des Fernsehens...* E. V. Ballin

Film as folk museum: authenticity and nostalgia in Edgar Reitz's *Heimat* (*NGS*) S. Taberner

'Utopie Kino': Edgar Reitz' Beiträge zur Zukunft des Mediums. In: *Europäische Kinokunst im Zeitalter des Fernsehens...* M. Sobhani

Wilhelm Stekel's journalistic achievement, 1901-1914: the challenge to Therapeutic Nihilism (*Relation*) F. N. Clark-Lowes

Straub/Huillets Einleitung zu Arnold Schönbergs Begleitmusik zu einer Lichtspielscene – ein medialer Testfall. In: *Europäische Kinokunst im Zeitalter des Fernsehens...* U. Böser